CW01464314

Franklin
Executive
Vocabulary
for Effective
Communication
With Free Download MP3 File
of Words From CD #1

2180 Most Common Words
For Business Communication

For Free Download
MP3 File of CD #1
(link is on the last page of the book)

Franklin Vocab System

Support Email: FranklinVocab@gmail.com

You Only Get One or Two Important Meanings and "Short Memorable Sentence Fragments" (not too many meanings or long sentences)

You don't get 3 or 5 or 10 meanings and sentences that are impossible to remember (a dictionary is better if you want to do PhD on some aspects of words).

I give you a short and memorable sentence fragments, so you can remember faster and better. Here are some examples (please notice how easily memorable the sentence fragments are):

euphoria = elation, feeling of well-being or happiness
USE = in a state of euphoria

evade = to avoid
USE = don't evade taxes

excerpt = selection from a book, extract
USE = excerpt of a new book

illicit = unlawful, illegal
USE = illicit liquor

immense = huge
USE = at immense cost

de facto = actual
USE = de facto standard (Not full sentence)

draconian = harsh
USE = draconian laws

prodigy = a person with extraordinary ability or talent
USE = a child prodigy

eke = to add to, supplement
USE = to eke out a living

Herculean = powerful, large
USE = a Herculean task

pyrrhic = a battle won with unacceptable losses
USE = a pyrrhic victory

How is this Book Organized

This book contains the words, meanings, and memorable sentence fragments. The same are on the 11 CDs that you can download (for instructions on how to download, please forward Amazon purchase email to download@EFranklinVocab.com.

The words are given in bold (example, the words **belabor** and **buttress** below). The meaning is given after the equal sign (=) following a word.

The words are not necessarily in alphabetical order.

We have used the US spellings. The British spelling of a word, when different from the US spelling, is given in bracket after BRITISH as shown for the word **belabor** below.

USE gives a sentence fragment carefully chosen for memory. When no sentence fragment is given, a * is shown as in the word **buttress** below.

belabor (BRITISH = belabour) = to assail verbally, to insist repeatedly or harp on
USE = belabor a point

buttress = support
USE = *

Table of Contents

CD 1

amulet = ornament worn as a charm against evil spirits, talisman
USE = many people in villages wear amulets

analogous = similar, comparable, parallel
USE = Hypnotic trance is in a sense analogous to sleep

anarchy = absence of government or law
USE = there was anarchy after the government fell

animosity = dislike, hatred
USE = animosity between the teams

antipathy = repulsion, hatred
USE = He is a private man with a deep antipathy towards the press

apathy = indifference, lack of emotion
USE = the government's apathy during the accident was shocking

aperture = opening
USE = aperture of the camera

appease = pacify, satisfy
USE = they changed the law in order to appease their critics

append = affix, attach
USE = append a short footnote to the text

apprise = inform, to give notice of
USE = The President has been apprised of the situation

arbitrary = tyrannical, capricious, depending solely on individual will
USE = an arbitrary decision

arcane = secret
USE = the arcane details of the agreement

arduous = extremely difficult, hard
USE = an arduous journey

arid = dry, dull
USE = an arid climate

articulate = well-spoken
USE = an articulate speech

ascertain = discover, determine, make certain of
USE = to ascertain the cause of

ascetic = a self-denying, simple person
USE = Gandhiji lived as an ascetic

astral = pertaining to stars, exalted, elevated in position
USE = astral body

astute = wise
USE = politically astute

atrophy = the wasting away of muscle
USE = After months in a hospital bed, his leg muscles had atrophied

attenuate = weaken, to make thin or slender
USE = Radiation from the sun is attenuated by the Earth's atmosphere

attest = testify
USE = attested copy of mark sheet

augment = increase, expand, extend
USE = He would have to find work to augment his income

auspicious = favorable, promising
USE = auspicious start

austere = stern, strict, unadorned, harsh, Spartan
USE = an austere room

autonomous = Self-governing, separate, independent
USE = an autonomous university

auxiliary = secondary, supplementary, reserve
USE = an auxiliary nurse

avarice = greed
USE = Her business empire brought her wealth beyond the dreams of avarice.

averse = loath, reluctant, being disinclined towards something
USE = the actor was not averse to giving interviews

avert = turn away
USE = avert a crisis

balm = soothing ointment, soothing, healing influence
USE = a new skin balm

belabor (BRITISH = belabour) = to assail verbally, to insist repeatedly or harp on
USE = belabor a point

belated = delayed, overdue, late
USE = Belated birthday greetings

belittle = disparage, to represent as unimportant
USE = they attempted to belittle the leader

bellicose = Warlike, aggressive
USE = a bellicose situation

belligerent = combative, hostile
USE = his assistant was belligerent

benefactor = patron, someone giving aid or money
USE = king Ashoka was a benefactor

benign = kind, gentle, or harmless
USE = a benign ruler or benign tumor

boisterous = rowdy, loud, noisy, unrestrained
USE = a boisterous child

brevity = shortness of expression
USE = brevity in writing is an art

buttress = support
USE = *

cacophony = dissonance, harsh noise
USE = a cacophony of voices

calamity = disaster
USE = natural calamity

callous = insensitive, thick-skinned
USE = callous attitude

capacious = spacious, large, roomy, extensive
USE = a capacious handbag

capitulate = to surrender, submit completely
USE = the enemy capitulated

caustic = biting, sarcastic, able to burn, scathing
USE = caustic remarks

censure = condemn, criticize or find fault with
USE = His dishonest behavior came under severe censure

champion = to defend or support
USE = an Olympic champion

charlatan = quack, fake
USE = the charlatan was caught

circuitous = roundabout
USE = a circuitous route

clandestine = secret
USE = clandestine activities

claustrophobia = fear of enclosed places
USE = He suffers from claustrophobia so he never travels on underground trains

collateral = securities for a debt, or accompanying
USE = She used her house as collateral for a loan

colloquial = informal speech
USE = colloquial speech

commensurate = proportionate
USE = a salary that is commensurate with skills and experience

complacent = self-satisfied, smug, affable
USE = students shouldn't become complacent about studies

compliant = submissive and yielding
USE = a compliant child

concatenate = link, linked together
USE = *

concave = curving inward
USE = a concave lens

conciliatory = reconciling, overcoming distrust or hostility
USE = a conciliatory approach

concomitant = accompanying something, concurrent
USE = Loss of memory is a natural concomitant of old age

condone = overlook wrong doing, pardon, justify
USE = If the government is seen to condone violence, the bloodshed will never stop

conduit = pipe, tube
USE = a conduit for water to flow through

confiscate = seize, to appropriate
USE = the government confiscated the criminal's property

congenial = friendly, similar in tastes and habits
USE = a congenial company

congenital = inborn, existing from birth
USE = a congenital disease

conjugal = pertaining to marriage
USE = conjugal happiness

connoisseur = an expert, gourmet, a person with refined taste
USE = a connoisseur of art

conscientious = honorable, upright, careful and thorough
USE = a conscientious student

consensus = general agreement, unanimity of opinion
USE = to reach a consensus

consonant = harmonious, in agreement with
USE = *

🖉 **consummate** = perfect, having great skills, complete, accomplished
USE = a consummate professional

contentious = argumentative, quarrelsome, disagreeable, belligerent
USE = a contentious decision

contravene = oppose, to contradict, deny, act contrary to
USE = by accepting the money, she was in contravention of company rules.

convene = assemble (a group), to meet, come together
USE = the committee convenes three times a year

conventional = customary, standard, typical, commonplace
USE = a conventional wedding

convex = curving outward
USE = convex mirror

convoluted = twisted, complicated, involved
USE = a very convoluted route

copious = abundant, plentiful
USE = they drank copious amounts of wine

countermand = overrule, to annual, cancel
USE = the general countermanded the orders issued in his absence

🖉 **covert** = secret, hidden
USE = covert police operations

crescendo = becoming louder, gradual increase in volume of sound
USE = The music reached a crescendo.

criterion = a standard used in judging, rule for testing
USE = judged by financial criteria alone

cryptic = mysterious, puzzling
USE = a cryptic message

cursory = hasty, superficial
USE = a cursory glance

curtail = to shorten
USE = to curtain spending

dearth = scarcity, lack, insufficiency
USE = there is no dearth of talent in the country

debilitate = to weaken, enfeeble
USE = Chemotherapy exhausted and debilitated him

definitive = conclusive, final, clear-cut, explicit or decisive
USE = a definitive judgment

demise = Death
USE = demise of her mother

denounce = condemn, to accuse, blame
USE = they've been denounced as terrorists

depict = portray, to describe, represent
USE = Her paintings depict the lives of ordinary people

deplete = exhaust, to use up
USE = Alcohol depletes the body of B vitamins

deplore = condemn, to express or feel disapproval of, regret strongly
USE = a deplorable situation

deploy = arrange forces, to spread out strategically over an area
USE = to deploy my skills

destitute = very poor, poverty-stricken
USE = The floods left thousands of people destitute

detached = emotionally removed, separate, unconnected
USE = She seemed a bit detached, as if her mind were on other things

detrimental = harmful or injury
USE = a detrimental effect

deviate = turn away from, to stray, wander
USE = The recent pattern of weather deviates from the norm for this time of year

devoid = empty, totally lacking
USE = devoid of all comforts

devout = pious, deeply religious
USE = a devout Hindu

diabolical = devilish, fiendish, wicked
USE = Conditions in the prison were diabolical

diaphanous = sheer, translucent, allowing light to show through, delicate
USE = a diaphanous silk veil

dictum = popular saying, authoritative statement
USE = He followed the famous American dictum, 'Don't get mad, get even'

digress = ramble, to turn aside, to stray from the main point
USE = don't digress from the topic

dilapidated = neglected, in disrepair, run-down
USE = dilapidated buildings

dilate = enlarge, swell, extend
USE = dilated pupils

disarray = disorder, clutter
USE = The news threw his plans into disarray

disclaim = renounce, to deny, disavow
USE = the terrorists disclaimed responsibility for the bomb blast

discrepancy = difference between
USE = There is some discrepancy between the two accounts

dispassionate = Impartial, free from emotion, unbiased
USE = clear-sighted and dispassionate

disperse = scatter, to break up
USE = to disperse the crowd

dissemble = pretend, disguise one's motives
USE = He accused the government of dissembling

disseminate = distribute, to spread far and wide
USE = web sites are used to disseminate political propaganda

dissuade = to persuade someone to alter original intentions
USE = We tried to dissuade him from leaving.

diverge = branch off, to move in different directions
USE = their paths diverged

diverse = varying, differing
USE = unity in diversity

divest = strip, deprive, to get rid of
USE = The company is divesting its less profitable business operations

dogmatic = certain, unchanging in opinion
USE = a dogmatic approach to life

doldrums = dullness
USE = Her career was in the doldrums

dormant = asleep, at rest, inactive
USE = a dormant volcano

effigy = likeness, mannequin
USE = Crowds marched through the streets carrying burning effigies of the president

egregious = grossly wrong
USE = an egregious example of racism

egress = exit
USE = everyone rushed to the egress

emancipate = liberate
USE = emancipated women

embellish = exaggerate, make attractive with decoration
USE = He embellished the story with lots of dramatic details.

eminent = distinguished, famous, celebrated
USE = an eminent scientist

emulate = imitate
USE = emulate the success of others

enormity = large, tragic, state of being gigantic or terrible
USE = enormity of the situation

entice = to lure or tempt
USE = entice the customer into buying things

ephemeral = short-lived, momentary, fleeting
USE = his fame was ephemeral

equanimity = composure, calmness
USE = he replied with equanimity

equitable = fair
USE = a fair and equitable voting system

equivocate = make intentionally ambiguous
USE = She accused the minister of equivocating

erratic = constantly changing
USE = erratic power supply

erroneous = mistaken, in error
USE = an erroneous answer

erudite = learned
USE = erudite guest

esoteric = known by only a few
USE = an esoteric collection

ethereal = light, airy, spiritual, delicate
USE = ethereal beauty

etymology = study of words
USE = an interest in etymology

euphemism = genteel expression
USE = Passed away" is a euphemism for "died

evoke = draw forth, to produce a reaction
USE = evoke memories of childhood

exorbitant = expensive, greater than reasonable
USE = exorbitant prices

explicit = definite, clear
USE = explicit about one's plans

extort = extract, force
USE = to extort money

façade = mask, front, face
USE = the building has a new façade

facilitate = make easier, to aid, assist
USE = to facilitate the process

facsimile = duplicate
USE = facsimile machine is a fax machine

fallacious = wrong, unsound, illogical
USE = fallacious argument

fanaticism = excessive zeal, extreme devotion to a cause
USE = their fanaticism led to the fight

feasible = likely to succeed, possible
USE = a feasible plan

fiasco = debacle, disaster
USE = the dinner party was a complete fiasco

finesse = skill
USE = It was a disappointing performance which lacked finesse

foil = defeat
USE = The prisoners' attempt to escape was foiled

forensic = pertaining to debate, solving crime
USE = forensic evidence

frugal = thrifty
USE = a frugal millionaire

furor (BRITISH = furore) = commotion
USE = the furor over his last film

genteel = elegant
USE = genteel manners

grandiose = impressive, large
USE = grandiose ceremony

gratis = free, costing nothing
USE = I'll give it to you, gratis!

gratuitous = unwarranted, uncalled for, free
USE = gratuitous violence

gratuity = tip
USE = you give gratuity or tip to the waiter

gregarious = sociable, outgoing
USE = a gregarious person

gullible = easily deceived
USE = gullible people

homage = respect
USE = to pay homage

homogeneous = uniform
USE = homogeneous milk

humane = Compassionate
USE = humane treatment of prisoners of war

hyperbole = exaggeration
USE = The blurb on the back of the book was full of the usual hyperbole - 'enthralling', 'fascinating' and so on

iconoclast = on who attacks traditional beliefs
USE = he is an iconoclast

idiosyncrasy = peculiarity of temperament
USE = She often cracks her knuckles when she's speaking - it's one of her little idiosyncrasies.

ignoble = dishonorable
USE = an ignoble action

illusory = fleeting, unreal
USE = illusory statements

immaculate = spotlessly clean, free from error
USE = dressed immaculately

immobile = still, not moveable
USE = She sat immobile, wondering what to do next

immutable = Unchangeable
USE = immutable law

impasse = deadlock
USE = The dispute had reached an impasse, as neither side would compromise

impeach = accuse, charge
USE = The governor was impeached for wrongful use of state money

impediment = obstacle
USE = war is an impediment to progress of the country

implicit = Implied
USE = an implicit threat

impotent = powerless
USE = When your child is ill, you feel impotent

impromptu = spontaneous, without rehearsal
USE = impromptu speech

incarnate = having bodily form
USE = as devil's incarnate

incense = enrage
USE = I was so incensed by what he was saying I had to walk out.

incessant = Unceasing
USE = incessant rain

inclusive = comprehensive
USE = the price is inclusive of taxes

incongruous = out of place, absurd
USE = The new computer looked incongruous in the dark book-filled library

incorrigible = who cannot be reformed
USE = an incorrigible liar

incredulous = skeptical, doubtful
USE = incredulous spectators

induce = persuade, bring about
USE = They induced her to take the job by promising more money

inept = unfit, clumsy
USE = an inept comment

inert = inactive
USE = The dog lay inert on the sofa

inevitable = Unavoidable, predestined
USE = an inevitable war

infer = conclude, deduce
USE = What do you infer from her refusal?

infinitesimal = very small
USE = The amounts of radioactivity present were infinitesimal.

infringe = encroach
USE = They infringed building regulations

ingenious = clever
USE = ingenious solution to a difficult problem

initiate = begin, introduce
USE = initiate a discussion

inkling = A hint
USE = He must have had some inkling of what was happening

innate = inborn, natural
USE = his innate goodness

insatiable = never satisfied
USE = an insatiable appetite

insidious = treacherous, sly
USE = High-blood pressure is an insidious condition which has few symptoms

insolvent = bankrupt
USE = the company went insolent

instigate = incite, urge, agitate
USE = The government will instigate new measures to combat terrorism

integrate = make whole
USE = He seems to find it difficult to integrate socially

interpolate = insert
USE = interpolate the data

intractable = not easily managed
USE = an intractable problem

intrinsic = Inherent, internal
USE = intrinsic value

invalidate = disprove, to negate or nullify
USE = the new experiment invalidated the old theory

invincible = cannot be defeated, unbeatable
USE = Last year the company seemed invincible but in recent weeks has begun to have problems

irrevocable = cannot be rescinded, irreversible
USE = an irrevocable decision

itinerary = detailed plan or route of a journey
USE = The tour operator will arrange transport and plan your itinerary

jargon = specialized language
USE = computer jargon

jocular = humorous, playful
USE = a jocular comment

judicious = prudent, showing good judgment
USE = The letter was judiciously worded

juncture = point where two things are joined
USE = At this juncture

jurisprudence = philosophy of law
USE = a student of jurisprudence

kindle = arouse, inspire
USE = the exciting stories she read kindled her interest

kinetic = pertaining to motion
USE = kinetic energy

labyrinth = maze
USE = Finally, through a labyrinth of corridors she found his office

laconic = brief, terse, using few words
USE = She had a laconic wit

laggard = lazy person, slow, or old-fashioned
USE = laggards are the last ones to accept any change

lascivious = Lustful, lewd
USE = a lascivious smile

lassitude = lethargy
USE = they are blaming the company's problems on the lassitude of the managing director

latent = potential, present but hidden
USE = the latent artistic talents that many people possess

lavish = to give plentiful amounts of
USE = lavish gifts

libidinous = lustful
USE = they objected to his libidinous behavior

CD 2

lineage = ancestry
USE = She's very proud of her ancient royal lineage

listless = lacking spirit or interest
USE = The illness left him listless<u>hint</u>

livid = enraged, reddened with anger
USE = He was livid when he found out

lofty = high, elevated in position
USE = a lofty ceiling

lucid = clearly understood
USE = a lucid explanation

ludicrous = absurd, laughable
USE = a ludicrous idea

luminous = bright
USE = a luminous object

magnanimous = generous, kindhearted
USE = the manager was magnanimous in victory, and praised the losing team

magnate = a powerful, successful person
USE = a well-known shipping magnate

magnitude = greatness of size
USE = They don't seem to grasp the magnitude of the problem

maladroit = clumsy
USE = She can be a little maladroit in social situations

malleable = moldable, tractable, capable of being shaped
USE = Lead and tin are malleable metals

mandatory = obligatory, necessary
USE = mandatory drugs test

manifest = obvious, evident
USE = illness first manifested itself

mentor = teacher, wise adviser
USE = the child found a new mentor to excel him at cricket

mercenary = calculating, venal
USE = mercenary motives

metamorphosis = a change in form
USE = metamorphosis of caterpillar to butterfly

meticulous = extremely careful, precise
USE = meticulous preparation

militate = work against
USE = The slowness of the judicial system militates against justice for the individual.

millennium = one thousand years
USE = How did you celebrate the Millennium

minuscule = small
USE = two minuscule pieces of toast

misanthrope = hater of mankind
USE = *

misgiving = doubt
USE = misgivings about the new policy

misnomer = wrongly named
USE = It's something of a misnomer

mitigate = lessen the severity
USE = to mitigate the risk

momentous = of great importance
USE = a momentous decision

morose = sullen, gloomy
USE = a morose expression

mundane = ordinary, worldly
USE = Mundane matters

myopic = narrow-minded, near-sighted
USE = the myopic refusal to act now

nadir = lowest point
USE = The defeat was the nadir of her career

nebulous = indistinct, cloudy, vague
USE = a few nebulous ideas

nefarious = evil, vicious
USE = nefarious practices

nicety = euphemism, minute distinction
USE = We don't bother with all the social niceties here

nocturnal = pertaining to night
USE = Most bats are nocturnal.

nomenclature = terms used in a particular science or discipline
USE = nomenclature of organic chemicals

nominal = slight, existing in name only
USE = nominal fees

novice = beginner
USE = I've never driven a car before - I'm a complete novice

noxious = toxic, harmful
USE = a noxious smell

nuance = shade of meaning, subtlety
USE = Linguists explore the nuances of language

nullify = void
USE = the law was nullified

obscure = vague, unclear, dim
USE = His answers were obscure and confusing

obsolete = outdated
USE = Kerosene lamps became obsolete when electric lighting was invented

obviate = make unnecessary
USE = A peaceful solution would obviate the need to send a military force.

officious = forward, obtrusive
USE = an officious little man

ominous = threatening, indicating misfortune
USE = ominous dark clouds

Omnipotent = all-powerful
USE = an omnipotent king

omniscient = all-knowing
USE = the omniscient narrator

opaque = nontransparent
USE = opaque glass

opportune = well-timed
USE = an opportune moment

optimum = best condition
USE = an optimum choice

opulence = wealth
USE = he has only known opulence

oscillate = to move back and forth
USE = My emotions oscillate between desperation and hope

palatial = grand, splendid
USE = he owned a palatial house

panacea = cure-all
USE = Technology is not a panacea for all our problems

panorama = vista, broad view
USE = From the hotel roof you can enjoy a panorama of the whole city

paraphrase = restatement
USE = to paraphrase, what it means is

parity = equality
USE = pay parity

parody = imitation, ridicule
USE = he wrote parodies of other people's works

patronize = condescend, disparage, to buy from
USE = We always patronize Taj Restaurant - the food is so good there

paucity = scarcity
USE = a paucity of information

pedestrian = common, unimaginative
USE = he wrote page after page of pedestrian prose

penury = extreme poverty
USE = the painter lived in penury

perpetual = continuous
USE = in perpetual fear

perturbation = agitation, disturbance
USE = Perturbations in the orbit of the planet Uranus led to the discovery of Neptune

phobia = fear, anxiety
USE = a phobia of worms

pillage = plunder, to loot
USE = Works of art were pillaged from many countries

pinnacle = highest point of development
USE = the pinnacle of her career

pious = devout, holy, extremely religious
USE = a pious follower of the religion

placate = appease, to soothe
USE = Outraged minority groups will not be placated by promises of future improvements

podium = stand, rostrum, platform
USE = she stood on the winner's podium

ponderous = heavy, bulky
USE = a slow and ponderous manner

posterity = future generations
USE = to preserve for posterity

pragmatic = practical
USE = the pragmatic approach to problems

precarious = dangerous, risky
USE = precarious financial position

precipitate = cause, sudden and unexpected
USE = Fear of losing her job precipitated her into action

preclude = To prevent
USE = *

preeminent (BRITISH = pre-eminent) = supreme, distinguished
USE = pre-eminent scientist

premonition = warning
USE = She had a sudden premonition of what the future might bring

presumptuous = assuming, improperly bold
USE = It would be presumptuous of me to comment on this matter

pretext = excuse
USE = He came round to see her on some flimsy pretext

prevaricate = lie
USE = He accused the minister of prevaricating

pristine = pure, unspoiled
USE = pristine beaches

profane = impure, contrary to religion
USE = profane language

prolific = fruitful, productive
USE = prolific writer

propriety = appropriateness
USE = he was careful always to behave with propriety

prostrate = lying flat on the ground
USE = he prostrated himself before the god idol

protocol = code of diplomatic etiquette
USE = royal protocol

provincial = intolerant, insular, limited in scope
USE = provincial governments

proximity = nearness
USE = The best thing about the location of the house is its proximity to the market

proxy = substitute, agent
USE = a proxy vote

pseudonym = alias, pen name
USE = the author used a pseudonym

pundit = learned or politically astute person
USE = a political pundit

punitive = punishing
USE = punitive action

purge = cleanse, remove
USE = Party leaders have undertaken to purge the party of extremists

quack = charlatan, fake
USE = quacks operate eyes and at times cause blindness

quadruped = four foot animal
USE = cow is a quadruped

quarantine = detention, confinement, isolation period
USE = The horse had to spend several months in quarantine when it reached India

rail = rant, harangue, to complain angrily
USE = He railed against the injustices of the system

ramification = consequence
USE = Have you considered all the ramifications of your suggestion

rancid = rotten
USE = rancid oil

ravage = plunder, to destroy
USE = a country ravaged by war

rebuff = reject
USE = She rebuffed all suggestions that she should resign

recapitulate = restate, summarize
USE = finally the speaker recapitulated the main points

rectify = correct
USE = to rectify the situation

redress = restitution
USE = redress the problem

refurbish = remodel
USE = He refurbished the house inside and out

refute = disprove
USE = refute the allegations

reiterate = repeat
USE = reiterate the demands

rejuvenate = make young again
USE = take a vacation to rejuvenate

relinquish = release
USE = She relinquished her hold/grip on the steering wheel

relish = savor, to enjoy greatly
USE = I always relish a challenge

renounce = to give up or reject a right
USE = Gandhi ji renounced the use of violence

residue = remaining part
USE = The white residue in the bucket is a result of minerals in the water

resuscitate = revive
USE = Her heart had stopped, but the doctors successfully resuscitated her

retrospective = looking back to the past
USE = the change in law was retrospective

rhetoric = persuasive use of language
USE = election campaign rhetoric

rift = a split, an opening
USE = a deep rift in the rock

robust = vigorous
USE = a robust economy

saccharine = sugary, overly sweet tone
USE = I don't trust her, with her saccharine smiles

salient = prominent
USE = salient features of a product

sanction = approval
USE = His leave application was sanctioned

satiate = satisfy fully
USE = He drank greedily until his thirst was satiated

scion = child, descendent
USE = He's the scion of a very wealthy family

scrupulous = principled, fastidious
USE = A scrupulous politician

sedentary = stationary, inactive
USE = sedentary lifestyle

serpentine = winding
USE = the serpentine course of the river

sonorous = resonant, majestic
USE = a sonorous voice

spurious = false, counterfeit
USE = spurious liquor

squander = waste
USE = They'll quite happily squander a whole year's savings on two-week vacation

stagnant = stale, motionless
USE = stagnant sales

stalwart = pillar, strong
USE = a stalwart supporter

stint = limit, assignment
USE = He has just finished a stint of compulsory military service

stipend = payment, allowance
USE = During summer project, he earned Rs 2,000 as stipend

stringent = severe, strict
USE = stringent laws

subjugate = to conquer
USE = India was subjugated by the British for hundreds of years

subsequent = succeeding, following
USE = The book discusses his illness and subsequent resignation from the government

sumptuous = opulent, luscious, lavish
USE = sumptuous meal

supersede = replace
USE = this agreement supersedes all old agreements

surfeit = overabundance
USE = India has a surfeit of cheap labor

surpass = exceed, excel
USE = your success will surpass your friend's expectations

susceptible = vulnerable
USE = children are susceptible to diseases

synthesis = combination
USE = a synthesis of what is best in India and America

tacit = understood without being spoken
USE = tacit understanding

tactile = tangible
USE = a tactile quality

terrestrial = earthly
USE = terrestrial rights

tome = large book
USE = a tome on the subject

topography = science of map making
USE = *

tractable = docile, manageable
USE = The problem turned out to be rather less tractable than I had expected

transpire = happen
USE = No one is willing to predict what may transpire at the peace conference

truncate = shorten
USE = TV coverage of the match was truncated by a technical fault

ubiquitous = omnipresent, pervasive
USE = the ubiquitous denim jeans

unanimity = agreement
USE = it was a rare decision made with unanimity

unconscionable = unscrupulous
USE = They both drank an unconscionable quantity of wine in the party

undermine = weaken
USE = Criticism just undermines their confidence

unequivocal = absolute, certain
USE = unequivocal support

unimpeachable = beyond question
USE = a man of unimpeachable integrity and character

untoward = perverse
USE = untoward happening

unwitting = unintentional
USE = unwitting victims of

urbane = refined, worldly
USE = an urbane, kindly and generous woman

utopia = perfect place
USE = the place is a kind of utopia

validate = affirm
USE = validate a claim

verbatim = Word for word
USE = She had an amazing memory and could recall verbatim quite complex conversations

verbose = Wordy
USE = a verbose explanation

vernacular = everyday language used by ordinary people
USE = the vernacular press

viable = capable of surviving
USE = viable solution

virtuoso = highly skilled artist
USE = Ravi Shankar is a virtuoso sitar player

vivacious = lively
USE = a vivacious person

volatile = unstable, explosive
USE = volatile temper

voracious = hungry
<u>USE</u> = a voracious reader

vulnerable = susceptible, innocent
<u>USE</u> = I felt very vulnerable, standing there in snow without warm clothes on

waive = forego
<u>USE</u> = The bank manager waived the charge

wanton = lewd, abandoned
<u>USE</u> = a wanton disregard for safety

windfall = bonus, boon, sudden
<u>USE</u> = windfall profits

xenophobia = fear or hatred of foreigners
<u>USE</u> = I found no xenophobia in America

zealot = fanatic
<u>USE</u> = a religious zealot

zenith = summit, highest point
<u>USE</u> = at the zenith of his achievement

CD 3

anecdotes (<u>BRITISH</u> = anecdote) = story, usually funny account of an event
<u>USE</u> = a speech full of anecdotes

ardent = passionate, enthusiastic
<u>USE</u> = ardent believer

arsenal = ammunition store house
<u>USE</u> = The army planned to attack enemy arsenals

artless = naïve, simple, open and honest
<u>USE</u> = an artless businessman

ascend = to rise or climb
<u>USE</u> = They slowly ascended the steep path up the mountain

assert = affirm, attest
<u>USE</u> = He asserts that she stole money from him

asymmetric = uneven, not corresponding in size, shape, position
<u>USE</u> = a trendy asymmetric haircut

bent = natural inclination towards something, determined
<u>USE</u> = She has a scientific bent

bibliography = list of books or sources of information
<u>USE</u> = bibliography at the end of the book

bilateral = Two-sided
<u>USE</u> = bilateral agreement

biped = two-footed animal
<u>USE</u> = *

boon = blessing, something to be thankful for
<u>USE</u> = Guide dogs are a great boon to the partially sighted

bovine = cow-like
<u>USE</u> = a bovine virus

buffet = blow, strike or hit
<u>USE</u> = The little boat was buffeted mercilessly by the waves

buffoon = fool, clown
<u>USE</u> = he looked like a buffoon in the red and green suit

candid = frank, unrehearsed, fair
USE = candid opinion

cardiologist = physician who specializes in the diseases of the heart
USE = if you have a chest pain, see a cardiologist

coagulate = thicken
USE = The sauce coagulated as it cooled down

coffer = strong box, large chest for money
USE = government coffers

cohabit = live together
USE = cohabiting couples

commend = praise, compliment
USE = The judge commended her on her bravery

commission = authorization to perform a task, or fee payable to an agent
USE = Do you take commissions

commute = lessen punishment
USE = the commute takes him 30 minutes

compatriot = fellow countryman
USE = *

compelling = convincing
USE = compel someone to do something

compensate = make up for, to repay or reimburse
USE = Victims of the crash will be compensated for their injuries

composed = cool, self-possessed, acting calm
USE = She finally stopped crying and composed herself

compound = augment, composed of several parts
USE = Salt is a compound of sodium and chlorine

compulsive = obsessive, fanatic
USE = compulsive gambling

concede = yield, grant, admit
USE = the government did not concede to rebel demands

consign = assign, to commit, entrust
USE = they were consigned to a life of poverty

consolation = something providing comfort or solace for a loss or hardship
USE = If it's any consolation to you

consolidate = unite, strengthen, to combine, incorporate
USE = to consolidate a position

constrained = confined, forced, compelled, restrained
USE = The country's progress was constrained by a leader who refused to look forward.

contend = struggle, to battle, clash, compete
USE = three chess players are contending for the prize

cosmopolitan = worldly, sophisticated, free from local prejudices
USE = Mumbai is a cosmopolitan city

credulous = believing, gullible, trusting
USE = *

culprit = offender, guilty person
USE = who is the culprit

cumulative = accumulate
USE = cumulative effect of

decorum = protocol, proper behavior, etiquette
USE = to act with proper decorum

deface = mar, disfigure, vandalize, to mar the appearance of
USE = jailed for defacing the poster of the Presidenthint

defame = slander or disgrace
USE = The opposition party tried to defame the Prime Ministerhint

defer = postpone, to submit or yield
USE = I defer to your judgment.

delegate = authorize, to give powers to another
USE = As a boss you have to delegate

desist = to stop doing something
USE = The high winds are expected to desist tomorrow

deter = discourage, prevent from happening
USE = the security alarm will deter thieves from coming to this park

dilatory = procrastinating, slow, tending to delay
USE = dilatory tactics

dispute = Debate, to quarrel
USE = a bitter dispute

disrepute = disgrace, dishonor
USE = to fall into disrepute

distrust = suspect, disbelief and suspicion
USE = mutual distrust

divine = foretell
USE = a divine intervention

divisive = causing conflict
USE = divisive forces

donor = contributor
USE = a blood donor

editorialize (BRITISH = editorialise) = express an opinion
USE = *

egocentric = self-centered
USE = Babies are entirely egocentric, concerned only with when they will next be fed

empathy = compassion, sympathy, identification with another's feelings
USE = *

entrench = fortify, establish
USE = It's very difficult to change attitudes that have become so deeply entrenched over the years

enumerate = count, list, itemize
USE = enumerate the contents

eradicate = abolish
USE = eradicate poverty

escalate = intensify
USE = His financial problems escalated after he became unemployed

ethical = conforming to accepted standards of behavior, moral
USE = ethical problems

euphoria = elation, feeling of well-being or happiness
USE = in a state of euphoria

evade = to avoid
USE = don't evade taxes

excerpt = selection from a book, extract
USE = excerpt of a new book

excommunicate = to bar from membership in the church
USE = *

excruciate = torture, agonize
USE = excruciating pain

expansive = sweeping
USE = an expansive view from the window

extrapolate = infer, to estimate
USE = extrapolate a trend from a small sample

extremity = farthest point
USE = The wood lies on the southern extremity of the city

facility = skill, aptitude, ease in doing something
USE = His facility for languages is astounding

fluctuate = waver, vary
USE = Vegetable prices fluctuate according to the season

foreclose = exclude
USE = it foreclosed any chance of diplomatic compromise

forgo = relinquish, to go without
USE = She had to forgo her early desire to be a writer

forsake = abandon
USE = Do not forsake me!

founder = sink
USE = The boat foundered in a heavy storm, taking many of the passengers with it

geriatrics = pertaining to old age
USE = *

granular = grainy
USE = granular sugar

habitat = dwelling place
USE = destruction of wildlife habitat

hygienic = sanitary, clean
USE = It is not hygienic

illicit = Unlawful, illegal
USE = illicit liquor

illustrious = famous
USE = an illustrious political family

immaterial = irrelevant
USE = How you dress is immaterial for a written exam

immense = huge
USE = at immense cost

immerse = bathe, dip
USE = immerse something in water

impassioned = fiery, emotional
USE = to make an impassioned plea for something

imperative = vital, pressing
USE = it is imperative that I speak with him at once.

implant = instill
USE = He implanted some very strange attitudes in his children

imposing = intimidating, dignified
USE = an imposing figure

impressionable = susceptible, easily influenced
USE = at an impressionable age

impulse = sudden tendency
USE = a sudden impulse to shout

impulsive = to act suddenly
USE = Don't be so impulsive - think before you act.

inaugurate = to begin or start officially
USE = inaugurate a new shop

inconceivable = unthinkable
USE = It would be inconceivable for her to change her mind.

indulge = to give in to a craving or desire
USE = to indulge in a little nostalgia

inestimable = priceless
USE = The medical importance of this discovery is of inestimable value

infiltrate = to pass secretly into enemy territory
USE = A journalist managed to infiltrate the powerful drug cartel

infuriate = enrage, to anger
USE = His casual attitude infuriates me

integral = essential
USE = an integral part of

interrogate = to question formally
USE = Thousands of dissidents were interrogated

jaundiced = biased, embittered, affected by jaundice
USE = a very jaundiced view of life

keen = of sharp mind
USE = a keen interest

legible = readable
USE = his handwriting is barely legible

legislate = make laws
USE = *

legitimate = lawful
USE = The army must give power back to the legitimate government

lenient = forgiving, permissive
USE = They believe that judges are too lenient with terrorist suspects

linguistics = study of language
USE = *

logo = corporate symbol
USE = a corporate logo

malady = illness
USE = Apathy is one of the maladies of modern society

malice = spite, hatred
USE = There certainly wasn't any malice in her comments

marginal = insignificant
USE = a marginal improvement

martyr = sacrifice, symbol
USE = a religious martyr

matriculate = to enroll as a member of a college
USE = *

meager (BRITISH = meagre) = scanty
USE = a meager salary

melancholy = reflective, gloomy
USE = a melancholy piece of music

melodious = having a pleasing melody
USE = a melodious voice

monologue = dramatic speech performed by one actor
USE = *

negligible = insignificant
USE = negligible contribution

neutralize = offset, nullify, to balance
USE = to neutralize an acid

niche = nook, best position for something
USE = make a niche for himself

numismatics = coin collecting
USE = *

opine = think, to express an opinion
USE = Power grows from the barrel of a gun, opined Mao Tse-tung.

oracle = prophet
USE = Professor Jay is regarded as the oracle on eating disorders

oration = speech
USE = *

orator = speaker
USE = a skilled orator

orchestrate = organize
USE = a brilliantly orchestrated election campaign

ouster = ejection
USE = facing a possible ouster

pacify = appease, bring peace
USE = He pacified his crying child with a bottle

paradigm = a model
USE = to produce a change in the paradigm

paramount = chief, foremost, supreme
USE = of paramount importance

pathogenic = causing disease
USE = *

pauper = poor person
USE = *

pavilion = tent
USE = the West Pavilion of the General Hospital

pending = not decided
USE = The pending decision

perpetuity = eternity
USE = in perpetuity

phoenix = rebirth
USE = rose from the ashes like a phoenix

pilfer = steal
USE = He was caught pilfering from the shop

poach = steal game or fish
USE = to poach someone's ideas

porous = full of holes
USE = porous brick walls

posterior = rear, subsequent, bottom
USE = kindly move your posterior

predicament = difficult situation
USE = financial predicament

prescribe = urge, to recommend a treatment
USE = The drug is often prescribed for ulcers

prevalent = widespread
USE = These diseases are more prevalent among young children

procure = acquire
USE = He'd procured us seats in the front row

proficient = skillful, expert
USE = a proficient writer

progressive = advancing, liberal
USE = a progressive disease

proponent = supporter, advocate
USE = the leading proponents of

psychic = pertaining the psyche or mind
USE = psychic powers

quicken = revive, hasten
USE = to quicken the pace

radical = revolutionary, fundamental
USE = a radical thinker

rally = assemble
USE = an election rally

rapport = affinity, empathy, relationship of trust and respect
USE = to build rapport with someone

ration = allowance, portion
USE = no one was allowed more than their ration of food

rationale = justification
USE = the rationale behind some decision

rebuke = criticize
USE = He received a stern rebuke from the manager

receptive = open to other's ideas
USE = receptive to the idea

recount = to describe facts or events
USE = He recounted his adventures since he had left home

recruit = draftee
USE = to recruit volunteers

relent = soften, yield
USE = both sides refused to relent

remuneration = Compensation
USE = They demanded adequate remuneration for their work

renown = fame
USE = a woman of great renown

rent = tear, rupture
USE = There was a large rent in his parachute

repent = to regret a past action
USE = He repented of his sins

replicate = duplicate
USE = to replicate the original experiment

repress = suppress
USE = He repressed a sudden desire to cry

resolve = determination
USE = to strengthen your resolve for success

retain = keep
USE = She has lost her battle to retain control of the company

reticent = reserved
USE = the students were reticent about answering questions

retiring = modest, unassuming
USE = to be shy and retiring

revert = return
USE = the conversation reverted to money every five minutes

revoke = call back, cancel
USE = to revoke a decision

righteous = upright, moral
USE = a righteous and holy man

salutation = salute, greeting
USE = *

sanctuary = refuge
USE = a wildlife sanctuary

secluded = remote, isolated
USE = a secluded beach

sectarian = narrow-minded
USE = a sectarian murder

seismology = study of earthquakes
USE = *

sequel = continuation, epilogue
USE = the sequel of the movie Rocky is called Rocky II

sheepish = shy, timid
USE = a sheepish smile

skeptical (BRITISH = sceptical) = doubtful
USE = skeptical of his claims

sovereign = having supreme power
USE = a sovereign nation

spontaneous = impulsive
USE = spontaneous joy

stark = desolate, empty
USE = a stark room

stately = impressive, noble
USE = The procession moved through the village at a stately pace

stunted = arrested development
USE = stunted growth

subvert = undermine
USE = The rebel army was attempting to subvert the government

superfluous = overabundant
USE = superfluous comments

suspend = stop temporarily
USE = suspended for the day

syllabus = schedule
USE = Which books are on the syllabus this year

symposium = panel (discussion)
USE = a symposium on Indian cinema

synopsis = brief summary
USE = synopsis of her PhD thesis

tableau = scene, backdrop
USE = *

tactful = sensitive
USE = Mentioning his baldness wasn't very tactful

terminal = final, depot, station
USE = terminal cancer

thesaurus = book of synonyms
USE = a thesaurus in dictionary form

thesis = proposition, topic
USE = PhD thesis

tonal = pertaining to sound
USE = *

transitory = fleeting
USE = the transitory nature of life

unbridled = unrestrained
USE = unbridled enthusiasm

unfailing = steadfast, unfaltering
USE = her unfailing enthusiasm

unwarranted = unjustified
USE = unwarranted intrusions

utilitarian = pragmatic
USE = an ugly utilitarian building

voluble = talkative
USE = voluble praise

CD 4

analgesia = pain reducer
USE = analgesic

antagonist = an opponent, rival, adversary
USE = the antagonist was finally defeated

applause = acclaim, cheering, clapping, praise
USE = a round of applause

apprehension = fear, anxiety
USE = it's normal to feel a little apprehension before an exam

appropriate = to take or steal something
USE = appropriate someone's wealth

aspire = hope to achieve something
USE = aspire to be a cricketer

atrocious = extremely bad, wicked, monstrous
USE = atrocious weather or atrocious behavior

attainment = achievement
USE = *

audacious = Fearless, bold, daring
USE = an audacious claim

audible = Loud enough to be heard
USE = audible music

auditory = related to hearing
USE = the auditory areas of the brain

avenge = to take revenge or retaliate
USE = He swore he would avenge his brother's death.

ban = prohibition
USE = a ban on alcohol in Gujarat

beneficial = helpful, advantageous
USE = physical exercise is beneficial for your health

bereaved = suffering death of a loved one
USE = bereaved parents

bias = partiality, prejudice, slant
USE = biased opinion

bibliophile = One who loves books
USE = *

blaspheme = curse, profane, irreverent
USE = *

botanical = Connected with the study or cultivation of plants
USE = botanical garden

botany = The science of plants
USE = *

bouquet = a bunch of flowers
USE = gift a bouquet on birthday

cartography = the science or art of making maps
USE = *

celebrity = fame, widespread acclaim
USE = a film celebrity

certitude = assurance, confidence of certainty
USE = *

chaos = utter disorder and confusion
USE = The country's at war and everything is in chaos

chromatic = relating to color
USE = photo-chromatic sunglasses

circumference = The boundary-line of a circle
USE = the circumference of a circle

civil = courteous and polite
USE = He and his ex-wife can't even have a civil conversation

coerce = to force
USE = Employees said they were coerced into signing the agreement

cognition = understanding, perception
USE = it is important to learn about human memory and cognition

coherent = understandable, clear, logical, lucid
USE = coherent argument

concern = a matter of importance
USE = *

concerto = A musical composition for orchestra
USE = a piano concerto by Mozart

congress = formal meeting or assembly
USE = *

corrode = To ruin or destroy
USE = Steel tends to corrode faster in a salty atmosphere

cosmetic = related to the art of beautifying
USE = cosmetic surgery

credible = Believable, plausible
USE = credible evidence

defendant = person required to answer a legal suit
USE = *

deficient = Not having adequate supply, defective
USE = A diet deficient in vitamin D

deflation = decrease, depreciation
USE = *

deform = To disfigure, distort
USE = Age deforms the spine.

delineation = the act of representing pictorially, depiction
USE = *

delta = an alluvial deposit at the mouth of a stream
USE = the delta of the Nile

demotion = lowering in rank or grade
USE = demotion vs. promotion

denunciation = public condemnation
USE = *

dialect = regional style of speaking
USE = a regional dialect

differentiate = to distinguish between two items
USE = We do not differentiate between our workers on the basis of

diplomacy = Tact or skill in social matters, discretion
USE = It took all her tact and diplomacy to persuade him not to resign

disclose = reveal, to confess, divulge
USE = The police have disclosed that two officers are under internal investigation

discredit = to dishonor or disgrace
USE = discredited theories

disregard = pay no attention to
USE = complete disregard for

divert = to turn from one course to another
USE = to divert attention

dowry = property which a wife brings in marriage
USE = dowry deaths have not fully stopped yet

duration = The period of time
USE = of two years' duration

ecstatic = joyful
USE = an ecstatic crowd

effervescent = Giving off bubbles of gas
USE = effervescent vitamin C tablets

embezzle = to steal money in violation of a trust
USE = She embezzled thousands of dollars from the charity

endurance = ability to withstand hardships
USE = a test of human endurance

evict = to put out or force out
USE = Tenants who fall behind in their rent risk being evicted

exhilarate = To fill with high or cheerful spirits
USE = riding motorcycle is an exhilarating experience

explode = to disprove, blow up
USE = A bomb exploded

fabricated = constructed, invented
USE = a fabricated story

feud = a war between two people or groups
USE = a family feud

flag = to loose energy and strength
USE = The conversation was flagging

flounder = to falter, waver
USE = Although his business was a success, his marriage was floundering

forethought = Premeditation
USE = I had the forethought to make a copy of the letter

frivolous = Trivial
USE = I feel like doing something completely frivolous today

gestation = Pregnancy
USE = The period of gestation

gradation = A step, degree, rank
USE = the gradations of a ruler

hectic = hasty, hurried
USE = a hectic schedule

hemorrhage (BRITISH = haemorrhage) = heavy bleeding
USE = a brain hemorrhage

holistic = as a whole
USE = a holistic approach to disease

hypochondria = morbid anxiety about health, imaginary illness
USE = I thought the doctor was going to accuse me of hypochondria

hypocrite = One who makes false professions of his views
USE = He's a hypocrite

hypothesis = assumption subject to proof
USE = Several hypotheses for global warming have been suggested

impoverish = To make indigent or poor
USE = Excessive farming had impoverished the soil

indefensible = Untenable, unforgivable
USE = The war is morally indefensible

induct = To bring in
USE = was inducted into the party

industry = business or trade, energy
USE = *

inebriated = drunk, intoxicated
USE = inebriated state

inglorious = Shameful
USE = a long, inglorious record

ingrained = deeply established, firmly rooted
USE = The belief that you should own your own house is deeply ingrained in our society

inhabit = to occupy, to dwell in
USE = These remote islands are inhabited only by birds and small animals

inject = To introduce, as a fluid, by injection
USE = to inject himself with insulin every day

innumerable = Countless
USE = innumerable problems

insubstantial = lacking substance, insignificant
USE = insubstantial evidence

insufficiency = lacking in something
USE = *

intersect = To cut through so as to divide
USE = The roads intersect near the bridge

intrusion = entering without invitation; encroachment
USE = excessive government intrusion

invariable = Unchangeable
USE = The menu is invariable but the food is always good

juvenile = young, childish acting
USE = juvenile crime

kernel = A grain or seed, essential part
USE = a kernel of truth

larynx = organ containing vocal cords
USE = *

lethargy = indifferent, inactivity
USE = *

literal = word for word
USE = The literal meaning

locomotion = moving from one place to another
USE = *

luxuriance = elegance, lavishness
USE = *

malevolent = causing evil or harm to others
USE = I could feel his malevolent gaze

mannered = affected, artificial
USE = the actor was criticized for being very mannered

materialism = preoccupation with physical comforts
USE = we are becoming a self-centered society, preoccupied with materialism

medieval = relating to the middle ages
USE = a medieval building

metronome = time keeping device used in music
USE = *

monochromatic = having only one color
USE = *

monogamy = marriage to one person at a time
USE = *

monolith = large block of stone
USE = *

naïve = simple, ingenuous
USE = It was a little naive of you

narrative = account, story
USE = It's a moving narrative of wartime adventure

negligent = careless, inattentive
USE = the teacher had been negligent in allowing the children to swim in dangerous water

noble = illustrious, imperial, legendary
USE = a noble gesture

offshoot = branch
USE = an offshoot of

paradoxical = self-contradictory but true
USE = this statement appears paradoxical

paternity = Fatherhood
USE = paternity leave

peer = a person of the same rank or group
USE = peer pressure

penultimate = next to last
USE = It's the penultimate episode of the series tonight

pervasive = Thoroughly penetrating or permeating
USE = a pervasive smell of diesel

pervert = to cause to change in immoral way, to misuse
USE = Her ideas have been shamelessly perverted to serve the president's propaganda campaign

philanthropy = generosity to worthy causes
USE = *

phonic = related to the nature of sound
USE = *

pneumatic = related to of air or gas
USE = pneumatic brakes

polarized (BRITISH = polarize) = split into opposite extremes or camps
USE = The debate is becoming polarized

pompous = self-important
USE = He can sometimes sound a bit pompous when he talks about acting

pore = to study closely or meditatively
USE = She spends her evenings poring over textbooks

precision = state of being precise, exactness
USE = Great precision is required to align the mirrors accurately

preface = introduction to a book
USE = *

procrastination = Delay
USE = *

protrusion = The act of protruding
USE = It has a series of protrusions along its back

qualify = to provide with needed skills
USE = B.Ed. qualifies you to teach in any secondary school.

rapt = deeply absorbed
USE = The children watched with rapt attention

redundancy = Excess
USE = *

reflection = image, thought
USE = reflection in a pool of water

reform = Change for the better
USE = who will reform India's obsolete laws

regress = return to a former place or condition
USE = regressed to the mental age of a five-year-old

repeal = no further effect
USE = repeal a law

repel = repulse, disgust, offend
USE = She was repelled by his ugliness

resonate = to echo
USE = His voice resonated in the empty building

retract = To recall or take back
USE = retract an invitation

sap = diminish, undermine
USE = Constant criticism saps you of your confidence

scale = climb up, ascend
USE = The prisoner scaled the high prison wall and ran off

scarcity = not enough, insufficient
USE = the scarcity of skilled workers

scenario = plot outline, screenplay
USE = There are several possible scenarios

slight = Of a small importance
USE = a slight improvement

submissive = yielding, timid
USE = a quiet submissive wife

subtle = Discriminating
USE = a subtle shade of pink

superabundance = An excessive amount
USE = *

supposition = assumption
USE = based on pure supposition

testimonial = A formal token of regard, often presented in public
USE = I have thousands of testimonials from my students about how they benefited greatly

theology = study of God and religion
USE = *

theoretical = abstract
USE = theoretical physics

tolerance = capacity to respect different values
USE = religious tolerance

tranquil = Calm
USE = a tranquil rural setting

transcendent = Surpassing
USE = transcendent power

transcript = A copy made directly from an original
USE = Mysteriously, the transcript of what was said at the trial went missing

transgress = To break a law
USE = anyone who transgresses will be severely punished

unruffled = calm, not anxious
USE = For a man in imminent danger of losing his job, he appeared quite unruffled

uproarious = Noisy
USE = an uproarious debate

variable = changeable
USE = variable interest rate

withdrawn = introverted, remote, timid
USE = she became quiet and withdrawn and rarely went out

toxin = poison
USE = toxins cause diseases

trammel = An impediment
USE = *

transfiguration = a change, an exalting change
USE = *

transformation = a change in form or appearance
USE = I'd never seen him in smart evening clothes before - it was quite a transformation

translation = a change from one state to another
USE = A literal translation

trifling = of slight worth, trivial
USE = a trifling sum of money

trying = difficult to deal with
USE = I've had a very trying day at work

unadulterated = absolutely pure
USE = *hint

unappealing = unattractive
USE = *

unbending = inflexible, unyielding
USE = a stern and unbending politician

undaunted = resolute even in adversity
USE = The team remains undaunted, despite three defeats in a row

undocumented = not certified
USE = *

undulating = moving in waves
USE = undulating roads

unfettered = liberated, free from chains
USE = In writing poetry, one is unfettered by the normal rules of sentence structure

ungracious = rude, disagreeable
USE = *

unheralded = unannounced, unexpected
USE = *

unidimensional = having one size or dimension
USE = *

uniform = consistent and unchanging
USE = the walls and furniture are a uniform gray

uninitiated = not familiar with an area of study
USE = *

unpolished = lacking sophistication
USE = *

unscrupulous = dishonest
USE = an unscrupulous financial adviser

unsoiled = clean, pure
USE = *

unsolicited = not requested
USE = unsolicited advice

unswayable = unable to change
USE = *

untrammeled (BRITISH = untrammelled) = unhampered
USE = Self-governing schools are untrammeled by education authority rules

unyielding = firm, resolute
USE = unyielding in its demands

upsurge = an increase, rise
USE = An upsurge in violence

valorous = Courageous, brave
USE = *

vehemently = strongly, urgently
USE = vehemently denied

veneration = adoration, honor
USE = Gandhi became an object of widespread veneration

verdure = fresh, rich vegetation
USE = *

verified = proven true
USE = Under interrogation, she verified that the tapes were authentic

vermin = A noxious animal
USE = He thought all terrorists were vermin

verve = enthusiasm, liveliness
USE = She delivered her speech with tremendous wit and verve

vim = energy, enthusiasm
USE = At 87, she is still full of vim and vigor

vindication = clearance from blame or suspicion
USE = the victory is being seen as a vindication of their tactics

virginal = pure, chaste
USE = virginal innocence

virtue = conforming to what is right
USE = Patience is a virtue

vituperate = to abuse verbally
USE = *

void = not legally enforceable, empty
USE = The election was declared null and void

volley = flight of missiles
USE = a fresh volley of machine-gun fire

vortex = swirling, resembling a whirlpool
USE = I was sucked into a vortex of despair

vulgar = obscene
USE = a vulgar patterned shirt

waspish = rude, behaving badly
USE = a waspish tongue

waver = to show indecision
USE = my concentration began to waver as lunch approached

wayward = erratic, reckless
USE = *

weighty = important, momentous
USE = weighty matters

whimsy = playful or fanciful idea
USE = *

zoologist = scientist who studies animals
USE = *

CD 5

abbreviate = shorten
USE = Reader's Digest prints abbreviated articles

abolish = annul
USE = abolish the old law

aboriginal = indigenous
USE = aboriginal people

abridge = to condense, shorten
USE = Abridged version of a bookhint

abscond = to run away secretly
USE = the accused was absconding

abstract = theoretical, intangible, complex, difficult
USE = it is too abstract for me to understand

accessory = attachment, ornament; accomplice, partner
USE = bathroom accessories or an accessory to murderhint

accomplice = one who aids a lawbreaker
USE = the accomplice was also sentenced to jail

accord = to reconcile, come to an agreement
USE = a peace accord

accrue = to accumulate, grow by additions
USE = accrue vacations

acoustic = pertaining to sound
USE = an acoustic guitar

adage = proverb, old saying
USE = an old adage

adapt = adjust to changing conditions, accommodate
USE = India is adapting well to the computer age

adept = skillful
USE = She's very adept at dealing with the media

adhere = stick to or to follow without deviation
USE = adhere strictly to guidelineshint

adulterate = contaminate, corrupt, make impure
USE = adulterated food

adverse = unfavorable, unlucky, harmful
USE = adverse reaction to medicine

adversity = hardship
USE = cheerful in adversity

advocate = to speak in favor of
USE = Gandhiji advocated vegetarian food

aesthetic = pleasing to the senses, beautiful, or related to art
USE = aesthetic appeal.

affable = friendly, easy to approach
USE = an affable person

affidavit = sworn written statement
USE = submit affidavit

affiliation = connection
USE = political affiliation

affinity = fondness or similarity
USE = a natural affinity

agenda = plan, timetable
USE = a hidden agenda

aggregate = total, collective mass or sum
USE = I got 90% marks aggregate and 95% in Maths

agitate = stir up
USE = they continued to agitate for social rights

agnostic = not knowing whether God exists
USE = *

agrarian = relating to farming or rural matters
USE = an agrarian society

alias = assumed name
USE = Jawaharlal Nehru, alias, Chacha Nehru

alienate = estrange, antagonize
USE = to alienate someonehint

alleviate = lessen, assuage, relieve, improve partially
USE = take tablets to alleviate pain

allocate = distribute
USE = allocate work to people

aloof = detached, indifferent
USE = he seems arrogant and aloof

altercation = argument, noisy dispute
USE = the altercation ended their friendship

amass = collect
USE = amass enormous wealth

ambiguous = unclear, uncertain; subject to multiple interpretations
USE = an ambiguous statement

ambivalence = conflicting emotions; attitude of uncertainty
USE = ambivalence towards something

amend = correct
USE = to amend a law

amenities = courtesies, comforts
USE = public amenities

amnesty = pardon
USE = under the terms of the amnesty

amoral = without morals
USE = Humans, he argues, are amoral and what guides them is not any sense of morality but an instinct for survival.

analgesic = pain-soother
USE = a mild analgesic

analogy = point by point comparison
USE = he used analogies to make his point clear

animated = exuberant
USE = an animated conversation

annihilate = destroy
USE = a city annihilated by an atom bomb

annotate = to add explanatory notes
USE = the officer annotated the application before forwarding it

anomalous = abnormal
USE = an anomalous artery

antagonistic = hostile
USE = antagonistic towards all critics

ape = mimic
USE = the new building merely apes the classical traditions

apprehensive = anxious
USE = a bit apprehensive about

aptitude = ability
USE = personal aptitudes and abilities

archives = public records
USE = archive film

arrears = in debt
USE = rent arrears

aspirant = contestant
USE = an aspirant to the throne

aspiration = ambition
USE = political aspirations

assimilate = absorb
USE = the refugees have assimilated into the local community

asylum = place of refuge
USE = apply for political asylum

attribute = ascribe
USE = an essential attribute for success

attrition = deterioration, reduction
USE = a costly war of attrition

atypical = abnormal
USE = The sociable behavior of lions is considered atypical of the cat family

audacity = boldness
USE = It took a lot of audacity to stand up and criticize the chairman.

automaton = robot
USE = I do the same route to work every day, like an automaton

avatar = incarnation
USE = Sri Krishna is an avatar

avid = enthusiastic
USE = an avid cricket fan

avocation = hobby
USE = I am a rocket scientist, but music is my avocation

barrister = lawyer
USE = a barrister of law

benediction = divine blessing
USE = his presence was such a benediction

benevolent = kind
USE = a benevolent action

berserk = crazed
USE = go berserk

biennial = occurring every two years
USE = a biennial function

bleak = cheerless
USE = bleak future

bloated = swollen
USE = a bloated stomach

bravado = feigned bravery
USE = his bravado got him in trouble

caliber (BRITISH = calibre) = ability
USE = of high-caliber

camaraderie = fellowship
USE = a tremendous sense of camaraderie

capillary = thin tube
USE = capillary in hands

caption = title
USE = the photo with an interesting caption

carcinogenic = causing cancer
USE = cigarettes are carcinogenic

cartographer = mapmaker
USE = *

celestial = heavenly
USE = The moon is a celestial body

celibate = abstaining from sex
USE = *

cerebral = pertaining to the brain
USE = cerebral films

cessation = a stopping
USE = a smoking cessation program

chronic = continual
USE = a chronic disease

coercion = force
USE = police used coercion

collaborate = work together
USE = they collaborated on the project

comatose = stupor
USE = By midnight I was virtually comatose

commandeer = seize for military use
USE = *

commemorate = observe
USE = a ceremony to commemorate the independence movement

commiserate = empathize
USE = I began by commiserating with her over the defeat

compact = covenant
USE = They made a compact not to reveal any details

compatible = well-matched, harmonious
USE = This software may not be compatible with older operating systems

compendium = summary
USE = the Gardener's Compendium

compensatory = redeeming
USE = compensatory damages

comprehensive = thorough
USE = comprehensive insurance policy

concise = brief
USE = clear and concise

conclusive = convincing, ending doubt
USE = conclusive evidence

concoct = devise
USE = He concocted a story about working late at the office

concurrent = simultaneous
USE = three concurrent prison sentences

confidant = trusted friend
USE = a close confidant

congruence = conformity
USE = he demonstrated congruence of two triangles

contempt = disdain
USE = She's beneath contempt

contiguous = adjacent, abutting
USE = Rajasthan and Gujarat are contiguous states

contraband = illicit goods
USE = *

converge = come together
USE = The paths all converge at the main gate

conversant = familiar
USE = I'm conversant with the topic

converse = opposite
USE = a converse opinion

conviction = strongly held belief
USE = a lifelong conviction

cordial = friendly
USE = a cordial smile

coup = master stroke
USE = a tremendous coup for the local paper

credulity = gullibility
USE = the witch doctor took advantage of the natives' credulity

crux = gist, key
USE = the crux of the problem

culinary = pertaining to cooking
USE = culinary equipment

cumbersome = unwieldy
USE = cumbersome equipment

cynical = scornful of the motives of others
USE = many people have become cynical about politicians

dais = platform
USE = speaking from the dais

debacle = a rout, defeat
USE = The collapse of the company was described as the greatest financial debacle in the history

decimate = destroy
USE = populations of endangered animals have been decimated

decipher = decode
USE = to decipher someone's handwriting

defeatist = one who is resigned to defeat
USE = a defeatist attitude

delete = remove
USE = deleted from the article

deliberate = ponder
USE = deliberated the question at great length

delineate = draw a line around, describe
USE = The boundary was clearly delineated

delude = deceive
USE = don't delude yourself

derogatory = degrading
USE = derogatory comment

despicable = contemptible
USE = a despicable crime

despise = loathe
USE = He despised himself for being such a coward

deterrent = hindrance
USE = a nuclear deterrent

devotee = enthusiast, follower
USE = devotees of cricket

dilemma = difficult choice
USE = dilemma about whether or not to go

dire = dreadful
USE = dire consequences

discernible = visible
USE = discernible difference between things

discerning = observant
USE = a discerning customer

disgruntle = disappointed
USE = the passengers were disgruntled by the delay

disinclination = unwillingness
USE = disinclination to do any work

dismantle = take apart
USE = She dismantled the washing machine

dissertation = lecture
USE = Ph D dissertation

distortion = misinterpret, lie
USE = a gross distortion of the facts

diva = prima donna
USE = a pop diva

diversion = pastime
USE = watching TV is a diversion from studies

diversity = variety
USE = unity in diversity

divulge = disclose
USE = he would not divulge how much the pen cost.

document = verify
USE = legal documents

domicile = home
USE = domicile certificate

dubious = Doubtful
USE = dubious means

dynamic = energetic
USE = young and dynamic

eccentric = odd, weird
USE = an eccentric professor

effeminate = unmanly
USE = An effeminate man entered the room

effervescence = exuberance
USE = her natural effervescence made her look happy

efficacy = effectiveness
USE = efficacy of a drug

elaboration = detailed explanation
USE = This point needs greater elaboration

elusive = evasive
USE = Success, however, remained elusive for her

embezzlement = theft
USE = embezzlement of company funds

encompass = contain, encircle
USE = the new music tape encompasses a wide range of music

encroach = trespass
USE = drive to remove encroachments

endear = enamor
USE = She is unlikely to endear herself to her colleagues with such an aggressive approach

endorse = approve
USE = expected to endorse these recommendations

enhance = improve
USE = plants enhance the beauty of any place

ensue = follow immediately
USE = The police officer said that he had placed the man under arrest and that a scuffle had ensued

entomology = the study of insects
USE = professor of entomology

entrepreneur = businessman
USE = he left the job to become an entrepreneur

equable = even-tempered
USE = an equable climate

esteem = respect
USE = held in high esteem

evasive = elusive
USE = evasive replies

execute = put into effect
USE = execute a will

exodus = departure, migration
USE = exodus of people from villages to cities

expedite = hasten
USE = expedite reply

expertise = knowledge, ability
USE = expertise in law

exploit = utilize, milk
USE = exploit our natural resources

faction = clique, sect
USE = the left-wing faction of the party

falter = waver
USE = the conversation faltered for a moment

fanfare = publicity
USE = there was much fanfare

fauna = animals
USE = flora and fauna

fictitious = invented, imaginary
USE = a fictitious story

figment = falsehood, fantasy
USE = a figment of my imagination

finale = conclusion
USE = a grand finale

foresight = ability to predict the future
USE = she had the foresight to buy a house before the prices rose

futile = hopeless
USE = futile effort

gambit = plot
USE = a clever opening gambit

generic = general
USE = generic drugs

germane = Relevant
USE = a germane answer

gist = essence
USE = That was the gist of what he said

glut = surplus, excess
USE = cause a glut in the market

glutton = one who eats too much
USE = be a gourmet without being a glutton

gravity = seriousness
USE = the gravity of the situation

grudging = reluctant
USE = the grudging respect of her boss

hallucination = delusion
USE = auditory hallucinations

harass = torment
USE = stop harassing me

herbivorous = feeding on plants
USE = a herbivorous dinosaur

hirsute = bearded
USE = a hirsute individual with a heavy black beard

hue = color
USE = there are fish of every hue

humility = humbleness
USE = He doesn't have the humility to admit when he's wrong

husbandry = management
USE = animal husbandry

hybrid = crossbreed
USE = hybrid flower or hybrid seed

hydrophobia = fear of water
USE = *

imbibe = drink
USE = the dry soil imbibed the rains quickly

imminent = about to happen
USE = imminent danger

impending = approaching
USE = impending disaster

implement = carry out, execute
USE = The changes will be implemented next year

import = meaning, significance
USE = the visit is of no import

improvise = invent
USE = I hadn't prepared a speech so I suddenly had to improvise

inanimate = inorganic, lifeless
USE = an inanimate object

incentive = stimulus
USE = Tax incentive

incite = foment, provoke
USE = he incited racial hatred

increment = step, increase
USE = salary increments

indemnity = insurance, compensate against loss
USE = city will indemnify all home owners

indifferent = unconcerned
USE = indifferent attitude

indiscriminate = random
USE = an indiscriminate terrorist attack

inebriate = To intoxicate
USE = the inebriated driver

infamous = notorious
USE = infamous criminal<u>hint</u>

inherent = innate, inborn
USE = an inherent distrust of lawyer

inhibit = restrain
USE = This drug inhibits the growth of tumors

intelligentsia = the intellectual elite of society
USE = *

intervene = interfere, mediate
USE = The Central Bank intervened

intimate = allude to
USE = She has intimated that she will resign if she loses the vote

inverse = directly opposite
USE = in inverse proportion to

CD 6

ironic = oddly contrary to what is expected
USE = an ironic comment

irrelevant = unrelated, immaterial
USE = irrelevant to the present investigation

irreparable = cannot be repaired
USE = irreparable damage

junta = small ruling group
USE = military junta

juxtapose = to place side by side
USE = The exhibition juxtaposes Picasso's early drawings with some of his later works

kaleidoscope = series of changing events
USE = a kaleidoscope of colors

kindred = similar
USE = kindred spirit

kleptomania = impulse to steal
USE = he used to steal as he was suffering from kleptomania

languish = weaken
USE = After languishing in obscurity for many years

laudatory = commendable
USE = the laudatory comments by the critics

legacy = A bequest
USE = The war left a legacy of hatred

lethargic = drowsy, sluggish
USE = feeling tired and lethargic

liaison = relationship, affair
USE = a liaison officer

Lilliputian = very small
USE = the model was built on a Lilliputian scale

liquidate = eliminate
USE = he was able to liquidate his debts

loath = reluctant
USE = I'm loath to

lucrative = profitable
USE = lucrative business

luster (BRITISH = lustre) = gloss
USE = the rich luster of well-polished furniture

Machiavellian = politically crafty, cunning
USE = a Machiavellian plan

malaise = uneasiness, weariness
USE = the current economic malaise

malign = defame
USE = a malign influence

malignant = virulent, pernicious
USE = malignant cancer cells

mammoth = huge
USE = a mammoth task

mandate = A command
USE = seeking a fresh mandate

manifesto = proclamation
USE = election manifesto

maternal = motherly
USE = maternal uncle

matrix = mold or die, array
USE = the cast around the matrix was cracked

mediocre = average
USE = a mediocre school

memento = A souvenir
USE = a memento of our holiday

mercantile = commercial
USE = mercantile system of accounting

meteoric = swift
USE = a meteoric rise to fame

methodical = systematic, careful
USE = a very methodical person

milieu = environment
USE = the social and cultural milieu

militant = combative
USE = a militant group

mirage = illusion
USE = For her, victory was just a distant mirage

mogul = powerful person
USE = industry moguls

moratorium = postponement
USE = a moratorium on nuclear weapons testing

motif = theme
USE = a flower motif

mutilate = maim
USE = the body had been mutilated beyond recognition

narcissism = self-love
USE = seem to suffer from narcissism

nepotism = favoritism
USE = guilty of nepotism and corruption

nexus = link
USE = there is no nexus between these two events

nirvana = bliss
USE = Buddha achieved nirvana

notorious = wicked, widely known
USE = a notorious criminal

novel = new, unique
USE = a novel idea

nurture = nourish, foster
USE = a carefully nurtured garden

obese = fat
USE = doctors advise the obese people to lose weight

objective = unbiased, goal
USE = my objective is to help you

obligatory = required
USE = The medical examination was obligatory

obtrusive = forward, meddlesome
USE = The logo was still visible but less obtrusive in light blue

Occident = the West
USE = *

occult = mystical
USE = occult powers

odyssey = journey
USE = a film about one man's odyssey

oligarchy = aristocracy
USE = *

onslaught = attack
USE = the forces could withstand an enemy onslaught

opiate = narcotic, sleep producer, pain reducer
USE = *

optional = elective
USE = optional subjects

ordinance = law
USE = a city ordinance

orient = align
USE = to orient yourself

ornate = lavishly decorated
USE = an ornate ceiling and gold mirrors

ornithology = study of birds
USE = *

orthodox = conventional
USE = orthodox medicine

ostracize = ban
USE = His colleagues ostracized him

pachyderm = thick skinned animal, elephant
USE = *

painstaking = taking great care
USE = painstaking research

parable = allegory
USE = the wise man told parables

parameter = limit
USE = keep within the parameters

paraphernalia = equipment
USE = cricket paraphernalia

parlance = local speech
USE = in common parlance

partial = incomplete
USE = partial withdrawal of troops

partiality = bias
USE = there was no evidence of partiality in the selection process

pathetic = pitiful
USE = a pathetic sight

peon = common worker
USE = an office peon

periphery = outer boundary
USE = the periphery of the city center

permeate = spread throughout
USE = permeated every section of society

perpetrate = commit
USE = to perpetrate atrocities against innocent people

perquisite = reward, bonus
USE = On getting promoted, he got a car as a perquisite

personable = charming
USE = he is personable

pervade = permeate
USE = The film is a reflection of the violence that pervades the society

philanthropist = altruist
USE = a wealthy philanthropist

plagiarize = pirate, counterfeit
USE = The book contains numerous plagiarized passages

plenary = full
USE = a plenary session

polygamist = one who has many wives
USE = *

posthumous = after death
USE = a posthumous award

postulate = supposition, premise
USE = Einstein postulated the theory of relativity

potion = brew
USE = a magic potion

potpourri = medley
USE = a potpourri of arts and media reports

precedent = an act that serves as an example
USE = There are several precedents for

precise = accurate, detailed
USE = precise location

predecessor = one who proceeds
USE = My predecessor worked in this job for twelve years

preempt (BRITISH = pre-empt) = commandeer
USE = in order to pre-empt criticism

prelude = introduction
USE = a prelude to wide-ranging reforms

prestige = reputation, renown
USE = international prestige

prevail = triumph
USE = common sense will prevail in the end

privy = aware of private matters
USE = privy to conversations

probe = examine
USE = The article probes the causes of

promiscuous = sexually indiscreet
USE = promiscuous in his youth

prone = inclined, predisposed
USE = prone to disease

protege = ward, pupil
USE = his young protégé

provoke = incite
USE = was provoked into the argument

pulsate = throb
USE = The whole room was pulsating with music

puny = weak, small
USE = My car only has a puny little engine

qualified = limited
USE = I'd like to qualify my criticisms

queue = line
USE = a queue at the cinema hall

rebuttal = replay, counterargument
USE = She issued a point-by-point rebuttal of the company's accusations

recipient = one who receives
USE = a recipient of the Bharat Ratna award

reciprocal = mutual, return in kind
USE = reciprocal support

reconcile = adjust, balance
USE = It is difficult to reconcile science and religion

recourse = appeal, resort
USE = without recourse to litigation

regime = a government
USE = the former Communist regime

remedial = corrective
USE = remedial classes

repertoire = stock of works
USE = an extensive repertoire

replenish = refill
USE = the supplies were replenished daily

replica = copy
USE = exact replica of the original

reputed = supposed
USE = She is reputed to be 25 years younger than her husband

requisite = Necessary
USE = the requisite skills

reserve = self control
USE = reserved nature

resolution = determination
USE = He showed great resolution in facing the robbers

resonant = reverberating
USE = a deep resonant voice

sadist = one who takes pleasure in hurting others
USE = the school teacher was a sadist

saga = story
USE = an ongoing saga of marriage problems

saline = salty
USE = saline solution

satire = ridicule
USE = political satire

saturate = soak
USE = The grass had been saturated by overnight rain

scapegoat = one who takes blame for others
USE = The captain was made a scapegoat for the team's failure

sensuous = appealing to the senses
USE = the sensuous feel of the silk sheets

severance = division
USE = a severance agreement

sham = pretense
USE = a sham marriage

shambles = disorder
USE = Our economy is in a shambles

shrewd = clever
USE = a shrewd politician

sibling = brother or sister
USE = sibling rivalry

simile = figure of speech
USE = the poem contains a simile

sinister = Evil
USE = sinister-looking man

spectrum = range
USE = The colors of the spectrum

stamina = vigor, endurance
USE = a great test of stamina

subservient = servile, submissive
USE = a subservient role

subsidiary = subordinate
USE = a subsidiary role

superimpose = cover, place on top of
USE = a picture of a dove superimposed on a battle scene

supine = Lying on the back
USE = supine posture

surrogate = substitute
USE = a surrogate child

surveillance = close watch
USE = surveillance cameras.

symmetry = harmony, congruence
USE = a pleasing symmetry

tautological = repetitious
USE = *

terminology = nomenclature
USE = scientific terminology

throttle = choke
USE = Sometimes he annoys me so much that I could throttle him

titillate = arouse
USE = So many adverts nowadays are designed to titillate

transcribe = write a copy
USE = the conversations were transcribed by typists

transgression = trespass, offense
USE = Who is supposed to have committed these transgressions

traverse = cross
USE = he traversed the continent from west to east

treatise = book, dissertation
USE = a six-volume treatise on patent law

trek = journey
USE = trekking through forests

ulterior = hidden, covert
USE = an ulterior motive

ultimatum = demand
USE = He gave her an ultimatum

uncanny = mysterious, inexplicable
USE = an uncanny resemblance

ungainly = awkward
USE = Ducks are ungainly on land

unilateral = action taken by only one party
USE = unilateral nuclear disarmament

unison = together
USE = Try to sing in unison

unmitigated = complete, harsh
USE = an unmitigated disaster

unprecedented = without previous occurrence
USE = environmental destruction on an unprecedented scale

upshot = result
USE = The upshot of the discussions is that

venue = location
USE = The hotel is an ideal venue

vogue = fashion, chic
USE = this style is in vogue

warrant = justification
USE = it did not warrant such severe punishment

CD 7

abstinence = Self denial
USE = observe abstinence

abusive = using harsh words or ill treatment
USE = abusive father

accelerate = To move faster
USE = accelerate your car

accessible = find, approachable
USE = such information is accessible to the general public

acknowledge = to recognize or accept
USE = acknowledged expert

adorn = to decorate
USE = the room was adorned with flowers

advert = advertisement, refer to
USE = since you advert to this matter frequently, it must be important

affirm = to assert confidently, testify
USE = the speech affirmed government's commitment to education

affluence = abundant supply of money
USE = the child had only seen affluence

agglomeration = collection, heap
USE = agglomeration of miscellaneous items

albeit = although, even if
USE = he tried, albeit without success

alchemy = chemistry of changing base metals to gold in old ages
USE = *

alimony = the money paid by a man to his wife after their divorce
USE = *

alloy = a mixture as of metals
USE = something made of alloy

altruist = One who practices altruism
USE = Gandhi ji was an altruist

ambidextrous = able to use both hands equally well
<u>USE</u> = an ambidextrous painter

amicable = Done in a friendly spirit
<u>USE</u> = an amicable agreement

amnesia = the loss of memory
<u>USE</u> = suffering from amnesia

amputate = To remove by cutting, as a limb
<u>USE</u> = his leg had to be amputated

anemia (<u>BRITISH</u> = anaemia) = Deficiency of blood or red corpuscles
<u>USE</u> = suffering from anemia, he looked pale

anesthetic (<u>BRITISH</u> = anaesthetic) = producing loss of sensation
<u>USE</u> = anesthetic medicine

anonymous = Of unknown authorship
<u>USE</u> = an anonymous letter

antagonism = Mutual opposition
<u>USE</u> = don't take antagonism personally

anthropologist = student of the history and science of human kind
<u>USE</u> = the anthropologist uncovered ancient human remains

anticlimax = change from what was expected
<u>USE</u> = death of the hero in the movie was an anticlimax

antiseptic = Anything that destroys the growth of micro-organisms
<u>USE</u> = antiseptic is used on wounds

apprehend = arrest
<u>USE</u> = police apprehended the thief

appropriate = suitable for a particular situation or person
<u>USE</u> = is this dress appropriate for the party

arrogant = believing one is better than other people
<u>USE</u> = arrogant behavior

asteroid = small planet
<u>USE</u> = *

astigmatism = an eye defect leading to improper focusing
<u>USE</u> = *

atheist = one who does not believe in god
<u>USE</u> = a confirmed atheist

atrocity = Great cruelty or reckless wickedness
USE = Soldiers sometimes commit atrocities against civilians

authentic = real or true
USE = authentic painting

authoritative = authentic, official
USE = an authoritative guide

autopsy = examination of a dead body by dissection
USE = They performed an autopsy

awe = reverential wonder or fear
USE = awe-inspiring, awestruck

babble = to talk foolishly or murmur
USE = he was just babbling

bait = food offered to fish to catch them; anything offered as part of a trap
USE = a mouse trap baited with cheese

beneficiary = One who is lawfully entitled to proceeds of an estate or property
USE = Her husband was the chief beneficiary of her will

bizarre = odd, fantastic
USE = a bizarre incident

bland = boring or without taste
USE = The food was bland

blunder = a mistake
USE = it was a big blunder

braggart = someone who boasts
USE = *

breadth = width
USE = *

bristle = a short, stiff hair or to show annoyance
USE = She bristled at the suggestion that it was her fault

brochure = a pamphlet
USE = a product brochure

bullion = gold and silver in the shape of rods or bars
USE = *

bureaucracy = too many people in an organization
USE = the university's bureaucracy

calligraphy = art of beautiful writing
USE = *

carat = a unit of weight used for gems
USE = a one carat diamond

carnage = massacre
USE = a scene of dreadful carnage.

casualty = serious accident or disaster
USE = The rebels suffered heavy casualties

cataract = Opacity of the lens of the eye resulting in complete or partial blindness
USE = cataract operation

catastrophe = Any great and sudden calamity
USE = natural catastrophe

centigrade = a unit of measuring temperature
USE = *

centrifugal = radiating, departing from the center
USE = centrifugal force

centurion = A captain of one hundred soldiers in the ancient Roman
USE = *

ceremonious = Observant of ritual
USE = ceremonious and polite behavior

chameleon = changeable in appearance
USE = like a chameleon, he assumed the political thinking of every group he met

charisma = a natural power which some people have to influence or attract people
USE = a charismatic leader

chassis = framework and working parts of an automobile
USE = chassis of a car

checkered (BRITISH = chequered) = marked by changes in fortune
USE = a checkered career

choreography = art of dancing
USE = *

cite = To refer to specifically
USE = to cite a case

clamber = to climb somewhere with difficulty, especially using your hands and feet
USE = The children clambered into the boat

cliché = an overused expression
USE = *

clientele = clients
USE = *

coincident = Taking place at the same time
USE = it was just a coincidence

combustible = something that burns easily
USE = combustible liquid

compilation = collection
USE = *

compliance = submission, obedience
USE = the design of school building has to be in compliance with the local building code

component = part
USE = computer components

compromise = agree to something which is not exactly what you want
USE = We need to reach a compromise over this issue

compute = to calculate
USE = Compute the ratio

conceit = Self-flattering opinion
USE = The conceit of that man is incredible

concentric = having a common center
USE = concentric circles

conception = beginning, forming of an idea
USE = at conception of the idea

concession = something that you agree to do or give to someone in order to end an argument
USE = Both sides will have to make concessions

conformity = behave according to normal standards
USE = there is too much conformity in this school

conglomeration = mass of material sticking together
USE = *

connotation = the implication of some term, not the literary meaning
USE = foreigners are usually unaware of the connotations of the words they use

conspiracy = when a group of people secretly plan to do something bad or illegal
USE = a conspiracy to overthrow the government

contaminate = To pollute
USE = contaminated water

contest = to dispute or to compete
USE = the defeated candidate contested the election results

context = relating to a particular thing or event
USE = in the context of

conveyance = transportation
USE = public conveyance

corrosive = causing gradual decay
USE = a highly corrosive acid

cosmic = related to the universe
USE = cosmic rays

counterpart = a person or thing which has the same purpose
USE = the prime minister is to meet his counterpart during the visit

couple = join, unite
USE = *

courier = messenger
USE = courier service

cubicle = small chamber
USE = office cubicles

cursive = Writing in which the letters are joined together
USE = cursive writing

deadlock = standstill, stalemate
USE = *

debris = wreckage, ruins, rubbish
USE = *

decelerate = slow down
USE = decelerate vs. accelerate

decomposition = decay
USE = Despite the body's decomposition, the police were able to identify the murdered man

decoy = Anything that allures into danger or temptation
USE = decoys are commonly used for hunting

default = The neglect or omission of a legal requirement
USE = to default on their mortgage repayments

degraded = lowered in rank, debased
USE = the degraded man spoke only of his past glory

demotic = related to the people
USE = a demotic society

detraction = slandering, aspersion
USE = he is offended by your detraction of his ability as a leader

devious = Out of the common or regular track
USE = a devious scheme

diffusion = Dispersion
USE = the process of diffusion in gases

diligence = Careful effort
USE = She hoped that her diligence would be noticed at work

dilute = To make fluid less concentrated by mixing
USE = Dilute the juice with water

discount = disregard
USE = we discounted what he had to say about his old company

discrimination = ability to see differences, prejudice
USE = *

dissection = cutting in pieces
USE = In biology classes at school we used to dissect frogs

distant = reserved or aloof, cold in manner
USE = his distant greeting made me feel unwelcome

eccentricity = Idiosyncrasy
USE = the eccentricity of the genius

ecologist = person who studies the relationship between living things and their environment
USE = the ecologist opposed the new dam

ecstasy = Rapturous excitement or exaltation
USE = they were in ecstasy

effectual = Efficient
USE = a real and effectual understanding

effervesce = To bubble up
USE = *

egoism = to think only about yourself
USE = the actor's egoism

egotism = Self-conceit
USE = the actor's egotism

ejaculation = exclamation
USE = *

elixir = cure-all, something invigorating
USE = *

embed = enclose, place in something
USE = *

empirical = based only on experience, inductive
USE = empirical evidence

energize = invigorate, make forceful and active
USE = *

entrance = put under a spell, carry away with emotion
USE = he was entranced by the stage magician

environ = enclose, surround in medieval days
USE = in old times, Delhi was environed by a wall

equilibrium = A state of balance
USE = the country's economic equilibrium

erotic = related to passionate love
USE = an erotic novel

erudition = Extensive knowledge of
USE = they respected his erudition

espionage = surveillance, observation, reconnaissance
USE = the government developed a system of espionage

esprit de corps = a deep loyalty of members towards the group
USE = the NCC cadets are proud of their esprit de corps

ethnic = racial, tribal
USE = ethnic groups

exchequer = government department in charge of the revenues
USE = *

exertion = effort, expenditure of much physical work
USE = the exertion spent in unscrewing the rusty bolt left her exhausted

extradition = transfer of an accused from one country to another
USE = an extradition treaty

faculty = mental or bodily powers, teaching staff
USE = mental faculties

fancied = imagined, unreal
USE = fancied insults

fanciful = whimsical, visionary
USE = this is a fanciful scheme because it does not consider the facts

fantastic = unreal, grotesque, whimsical
USE = your fears are fantastic because the moon will not fall on the earth

farce = broad comedy, mockery
USE = the interview degenerated into a farce

finite = limited
USE = a finite amount of time

flourish = grow well, prosper, make sweeping gestures
USE = the orange trees flourished in the sun

fluctuation = Frequent irregular change back and forth
USE = fluctuations in share prices

fluency = smoothness of speech
USE = you speak English with fluency and ease

foolhardy = rash
USE = don't be foolhardy, better take advise of the experts

formality = adherence to established rules or procedures
USE = signing this letter is just a formality

formidable = Difficult to accomplish
USE = a formidable task

franchise = privilege, commercial franchise
USE = the city issued a franchise to the company

friction = clash in opinion, rubbing against
USE = let us try to avoid friction in our group

frigid = Lacking warmth
USE = a frigid environment

frustrate = thwart, defeat
USE = we must frustrate their plan to take over the company

functionary = An official
USE = a government functionary

gait = manner of walking
USE = He walked with a slow stiff gait

gaudy = excessively bright, vulgarly showy
USE = her gaudy taste in clothes appalled us

generality = most
USE = the generality of young people

giddy = dizzy
USE = feeling giddy

glaze = to polish, burnish, glimmer, gloss
USE = glazed tiles

glossary = brief explanation of words used in the text
USE = see this word in the glossary

glossy = smooth and shining
USE = a glossy surface

gourmet = an epicure, a person with very fine taste of food
USE = gourmet restaurant

graphic = related to the art of delineating, vividly described
USE = graphic design

gratify = To please, or satisfy a desire or need
USE = He was gratified to see how well his students had done

grotesque = strange and unpleasant
USE = grotesque figures.

grueling (BRITISH = gruelling) = severe, tough, arduous
USE = grueling work

haphazard = random, accidental, arbitrary
USE = haphazard manner

hazardous = dangerous
USE = hazardous situation

hazy = slightly obscure
USE = hazy details

hierarchy = divided into ranks
USE = it was a strict hierarchy

hieroglyphics = picture writing
USE = *

hindrance = An obstacle
USE = I've never considered my disability a hindrance

hoax = a trick, practical joke
USE = he was embarrassed by the hoax

horticulture = the art of gardening
USE = *

hover = hang about, wait nearby
USE = the helicopter hovered over the helipad

hue and cry = outcry
USE = *

hurtle = to dash, to hurl
USE = the runaway train hurtled towards disaster

icon = An image or likeness
USE = Film heroes and heroines are icons for many young people

idiom = A use of words peculiar to a particular language
USE = To "have bitten off more than you can chew" is an idiom

illusion = An unreal image
USE = an optical illusion

illusive = Deceptive
USE = Their hopes of a peaceful solution turned out to be illusory

implication = that which is implied or suggested
USE = implications of your remark

imply = to communicate indirectly
USE = Are you implying that I'm fat?

inarticulate = unable to express clearly
USE = His speech was inarticulate

incidence = Casual occurrence
USE = what a coincidence-both of us are in this hotel

incompatible = unable to exist or work because of basic differences:
USE = we were incompatible as partners

incredulity = a tendency to disbelief
USE = a sense of incredulity, anger and pain

incur = bring upon oneself
USE = to incur debts

indignity = a loss of respect
USE = They were subjected to various indignities

indulgent = Yielding to the desires of oneself
USE = indulgent relative

inference = resulting conclusion
USE = what is the inference

inflate = enhance, heighten, raise, intensify
USE = his claims about the new products were inflated

innovation = change, introduction of something new
USE = she loved innovations just because they were new

insomnia = Sleeplessness
USE = he suffered from insomnia

intellect = the ability to understand and think in an intelligent way
USE = Her energy and intellect are respected all over the world.

interim = Time between acts or periods, temporary
USE = an interim solution

intimidate = To frighten or threaten
USE = he used to intimidate all the kids

intrude = To go unwanted to a place
USE = I hope I'm not intruding.

intuition = Instinctive knowledge or feeling
USE = base your judgment on intuition

invert = To turn upside down
USE = invert the dish

invulnerable = impossible to damage
USE = The command bunker is invulnerable, even to a nuclear attack

irrepressible = full of energy and enthusiasm
USE = Even the rain failed to dampen his irrepressible spirits

iterate = repeat, reiterate
USE = I will iterate the warning

jovial = Merry
USE = He seemed a very jovial chap

jubilation = Exultation
USE = There was jubilation in the crowd as the winning goal was scored

kiosk = a small stall for the sale of newspapers etc
<u>USE</u> = he bought a newspaper at the kiosk

CD 8

lagoon = a small lake, pond, basin
USE = we swam in the lagoon

lateral thinking = thinking which seeks new ways of looking at a problem
USE = Edward DeBono popularized the term "lateral thinking"

leeway = room to move, margin
USE = when you set a deadline, allow a little leeway

leniency = Forbearance
USE = The defending lawyer asked for leniency on the grounds of her client's youth.

lethal = deadly, fatal
USE = lethal weapons

lewd = sexual in an obvious and rude way
USE = a lewd suggestion

lexicographer = One who writes dictionaries
USE = *

libido = sexual impulse
USE = suppression of the libido

lieu = stead
USE = in lieu of

linguistic = related to language
USE = linguistic abilities

longevity = prolonged life
USE = To what do you attribute your longevity

lustrous = Shining
USE = long lustrous hair

mammal = vertebrate animal whose female suckles to its young
USE = humans are mammals

manipulate = operate with the hands, control or change by artful means
USE = he manipulated the results

mediate = negotiate as an agent between parties
USE = mediate between the two sides

meditation = to pay attention to one thing or religious reasons or relaxation
USE = prayer and meditation

merciful = Disposed to pity and forgive
USE = a merciful ruler

mesmerize = To hypnotize
USE = I was completely mesmerized by the performance

metallurgical = related to the art of removing metals from ores
USE = *

metaphysical = Philosophical
USE = metaphysical questions

metropolis = a big city
USE = a sprawling metropolis

migrant = Wandering
USE = migrant workers

mimicry = imitation
USE = she was mimicking the various people in our office

misadventure = An unlucky accident
USE = death by misadventure

miserly = stingy, mean
USE = a miserly person

missile = a flying weapon
USE = a missile launcher

mite = A very small amount
USE = I couldn't eat another mite

mobile = movable, not fixed
USE = mobile phone

mode = prevailing style
USE = mode of payment

modulation = toning down, changing from one key to another
USE = modulation of voice

molecule = the smallest particle of a substance
USE = a water molecule

momentum = An impetus
USE = give new momentum to their plans

monarchy = Government by a single ruler
USE = *

monetary = Financial
USE = monetary policy

monotheism = belief in one god
USE = *

monumental = massive, colossal
USE = a monumental task

moodiness = fits of depression or gloom
USE = the cause of her moodiness

multilingual = having many languages
USE = most Indians are multilingual

multiplicity = the condition of being manifold or very various
USE = a multiplicity of fashion magazines

nautical = related to ships, or navigation
USE = nautical miles

negation = denial
USE = negation of evidence

negligence = not giving enough care or attention
USE = medical negligence

nostalgia = sentimental longing for past times, reminiscence, recollection
USE = that song filled him with nostalgia

nutrient = nourishing substance
USE = nutrient food

obnoxious = Detestable
USE = he's loud and obnoxious

obsessed = consumed, fixated, gripped
USE = obsessed with career success

obstetrician = a doctor who delivers babies
USE = *

omnipresent = universally present, ubiquitous
USE = *

optician = One who makes eye-glasses
USE = *

optimist = person who looks on the bright side
USE = I am an optimist

optometrist = one who fits glasses to remedy visual defects
USE = *

orientation = act of finding oneself in society
USE = I attended the orientation program on my first day in the college

orthography = correct spelling
USE = *

oust = To eject
USE = The president was ousted in a military coup

palatable = tasteful, agreeable
USE = paying taxes is not palatable

pallet = small, poor bed
USE = straw pallet

parallelism = essential likeness, similarity
USE = there is a striking parallelism between the twins

paranoia = type of a psychological disease where a person thinks everybody hates him
USE = *

passive = Unresponsive
USE = He's very passive in the relationship

pathology = the study of diseases
USE = *

patriarch = the male leader of a family
USE = *

pendant = Anything that hangs from something else
USE = a beautiful necklace with a diamond pendant.

percussion = The sharp striking of one body against another
USE = Drums are percussion instruments

perturb = to worry someone
USE = News of the arrest perturbed her greatly.

perverse = Unreasonable
USE = a perverse logic

perversion = Diversion from the true meaning or proper purpose
USE = His testimony was clearly a perversion of the truth.

pessimism = belief that life is basically bad or evil, gloominess
USE = pessimism vs. optimism

plagiarism = The stealing of writing and publishing as one's own
USE = the editor recognized the plagiarism and returned the manuscript

plausible = Seeming likely to be true, though open to doubt
USE = a plausible explanation

podiatrist = the foot doctor
USE = *

potential = Anything that may be possible
USE = potential buyers

practicable = feasible
USE = not practicable to complete the tunnel soon

predatory = one that eats others
USE = The owl is a predatory bird which kills its prey with its claws

presumption = That which may be logically assumed to be true until disproved
USE = The presumption of innocence is central to Indian law

procrastinate = to delay, postpone, put off
USE = I'm just procrastinating the problem

protrude = To push out or thrust forth
USE = protruding ears

prune = to cut expenditure or branches, trim
USE = she pruned her manuscript into publishable form

psyche = soul, mind
USE = the psyche of people

psychiatrist = a doctor who treats mental diseases
USE = a psychiatrist often spends hours with a patient before making a diagnosis

psychosis = mental disorder
USE = *

pyromaniac = person obsessed with setting fires
USE = *

quietude = tranquility
USE = the monk lived in quietude of the jungle

ramp = slope, inclined plane
USE = ramps are built in hospitals so that people on wheel chairs can move easily

rationalization = bringing into conformity with reason
USE = She rationalized the expense by saying that the costly item would last longer

rebate = discount
USE = a tax rebate

recession = withdrawal, retreat, time of low economic activity
USE = The country was sliding into the depths of recession

recluse = One who lives in retirement or seclusion
USE = He is a millionaire recluse who refuses to give interviews.

recuperate = To recover
USE = recuperating after the operation.

recurrent = Returning at regular or stated intervals
USE = a recurrent nightmare

regeneration = spiritual birth
USE = modern penologists strive for regeneration of the prisoners

reimburse = To pay back an expenditure
USE = the company reimbursed me for the travel expenses

remunerate = To pay
USE = He is remunerated well and he works hard

renovate = To restore after deterioration, as a building
USE = He renovates old houses and sells them

renunciation = An explicit disclaimer of a right or privilege
USE = the renunciation of violence

repository = A place in which goods are stored
USE = libraries are repositories of world's best thoughts

repulsion = act of driving back, distaste
USE = the repulsion of the enemy forces

resignation = patient submissiveness, statement that one is quitting the job
USE = They received the news with resignation

responsiveness = state of reacting readily to appeals, orders, etc
USE = the audience applauded, delighting the singers by its responsiveness

restraint = controlling force
USE = an independent life, free of all restraints

resurgent = Surging back or again
USE = the resurgent militarism in the country.

retraction = withdrawal
USE = he dropped the libel case after the newspaper published a retraction of its statements

reverberate = to echo, resonate, resound
USE = the entire temple reverberated with the sounds of bells

rote = Repetition as a means of learning them
USE = rote learning

rubble = fragments
USE = The bomb reduced the house to rubble

rudimentary = Being in an incomplete stage of development
USE = Some unusual fish have rudimentary legs.

rusticate = banish to the country, dwell in the country
USE = I love the city life and can't understand how people can rusticate in the suburbs

ruthless = pitiless
USE = a dangerous and ruthless murderer

salvage = Any act of saving property
USE = gold coins salvaged from a shipwreck

sarcasm = Cutting and reproachful language
USE = *

satellite = the moon is a satellite of Earth
USE = *

scanty = meager, insufficient
USE = *

scavenger = animal which feeds on dead animals
USE = *

sedate = calm and relaxed
USE = The speed limit in many areas is a sedate 60 kph

senile = a lack of mental ability because of old age
USE = He spent many years caring for his senile mother

septic = putrid, producing putrefaction
USE = *

severity = harshness
USE = *

shackle = thing which hampers movement, bond, chain, handcuff
USE = *

shoddy = sham, not genuine, inferior
<u>USE</u> = shoddy workmanship

similitude = Similarity
<u>USE</u> = *

simulate = Imitate
<u>USE</u> = plastic is often used to simulate wood.

skeptic (<u>BRITISH</u> = sceptic) = One who doubts any statements
<u>USE</u> = *

skimp = provide scantily, live very economically
<u>USE</u> = *

slacken = slow up, loosen
<u>USE</u> = *

sleazy = flimsy, unsubstantial
<u>USE</u> = *

sleeper = something originally of little value or importance
<u>USE</u> = *

sophistication = artificiality, unnaturalness, act of employing sophistry in reasoning
<u>USE</u> = *

spatial = referring to space
<u>USE</u> = *

stalemate = deadlock
<u>USE</u> = the stalemate was finally broken

stellar = related to the stars
<u>USE</u> = a stellar explosion

stereotyped = over simplified, lacking individually, seen as a type
<u>USE</u> = *

subjective = occurring or taking place in the mind
<u>USE</u> = subjective experience

subsidy = direct financial aid by government, etc.
<u>USE</u> = food subsidy

subversion = An overthrow, as from the foundation
<u>USE</u> = He was found guilty of subversion and imprisoned

swindler = cheat
<u>USE</u> = the swindler was jailed

syllogism = logical reasoning where a conclusion is reached from two statements
USE = *

tantrum = attack of uncontrollable bad temper
USE = she threw tantrums

temper = moderate, tone down, or restrain, toughen steel
USE = *

terminate = to put an end to
USE = terminated the contract

tertiary = third
USE = *

thermal = Of or related to heat
USE = thermal conductivity

thrifty = careful about money, economical
USE = Indians are thrifty

torso = trunk of statue with head and limbs missing, human trunk
USE = *

touchy = sensitive, irascible
USE = a touchy issue

toxic = poisonous
USE = toxic waste

tract = pamphlet, a region of indefinite size
USE = *

trajectory = The path described by a projectile moving under given forces
USE = the trajectory of a bullet

tranquility (BRITISH = tranquillity) = Calmness
USE = I love the tranquility of the countryside.

transition = Passage from one place, condition, or action to another
USE = The health-care system is in transition at the moment.

transparent = Easy to see through or understand
USE = transparent Glass

trappings = outward decorations, ornaments
USE = *

traumatic = related to an injury caused by violence
USE = a traumatic experience from his childhood

tremor = An involuntary trembling or shivering
USE = There was a slight tremor in her voice.

tribulations = distress, suffering
USE = trials and tribulations

trilogy = group of three works
USE = *

turmoil = confusion, strife
USE = *

tycoon = a business magnate, baron, big shot, capitalist
USE = *

ultimate = Beyond which there is nothing else
USE = the ultimate luxury car

unearth = dig up
USE = *

unerringly = infallibly
USE = *

unfaltering = steadfast
USE = *

uninhibited = unrepressed
USE = *

unique = Being the only one of its kind
USE = a unique city

unruly = wild, with no discipline, defiant, indomitable
USE = an unruly crowd

vagabond = A wanderer
USE = They live a vagabond life

valedictory = relating to saying goodbye
USE = a valedictory speech

vampire = ghostly being that sucks the blood of the living beings
USE = *

vegetate = To live in a monotonous, passive way without exercise of the mental faculties
USE = children spend too much time vegetating in front of the TV.

velocity = Rapid motion
USE = high velocity

vendor = A seller
USE = a street vendor

ventriloquist = person who can make his voice appear to come from a different source
USE = *

verbalize = put into words
USE = *

verbiage = Use of many words without necessity
USE = verbiage explanation

verge = border, edge
USE = you are on the verge of a big success

vigilance = watchfulness in guarding against danger
USE = the vigilance of a neighbor

virtual = Being in essence or effect, but not in form or appearance
USE = virtual shopping

visionary = produced by imagination, fanciful, mystical
USE = he was a great visionary

wizardry = sorcery, magic
USE = *

worldly = engrossed in matters of this earth, not spiritual
USE = worldly possessions

zany = absurd, preposterous, mad, crazy
USE = *

CD 9

a la carte = priced separately
USE = from the à la carte menu

a priori = reasoning based on general principles
USE = a priori reasoning

abacus = counting device
USE = abacus was used for counting

abandon = desert, forsake
USE = The match was abandoned because of rain

abdomen = belly
USE = abdominal pain

abduct = kidnap
USE = abducted from his car

abide = submit, endure
USE = He abided in the jungle for forty days

abreast = side-by-side
USE = The motorcyclist came abreast of her car

abroad = overseas
USE = going abroad for studies

abrupt = sudden, unexpected
USE = the actor stopped abruptly

abstain = to refrain deliberately from something
USE = to abstain from alcohol

academy = school
USE = academy of arts

accentuate = emphasize
USE = Her dress was tightly belted, accentuating the slimness of her waist

acclaim = recognition, fame, praise
USE = an acclaimed author

accommodate = adapt
USE = we accommodated the needs of physically challenged

accredit = authorize
USE = accredited organization

accumulate = amass
USE = accumulate wealth

adaptable = pliable
USE = adaptable to change

adjacent = next to
USE = an adjacent building

adjourn = discontinue
USE = meeting was adjourned

administer = manage
USE = The country was administered by the British

admissible = allowable
USE = the new evidence was admissible

adversary = opponent
USE = main adversary

advise = give counsel
USE = His doctor advised him against smoking

aerobics = exercise
USE = She does aerobics

affiliate = associate
USE = my school is affiliated to CBSE

affluent = abundant, wealthy
USE = affluent neighborhood

aftermath = consequence
USE = in the aftermath of the explosion

aggravate = worsen
USE = his comments aggravated the problem

aggressor = attacker
USE = *

aggrieve = to afflict, distress, mistreat
USE = one aggrieved customer complained

aggrieved = unjustly injured
USE = He felt aggrieved at not being chosen for the team

agile = nimble, well coordinated
USE = agile child

agronomy = science of crop production
USE = *

air = discuss, broadcast
USE = game was aired live

alibi = excuse
USE = an alibi for its own failure

allot = allocate
USE = allotted seats on the front row<u>hint</u>

almanac = calendar with additional information
USE = a farmer's almanac

alms = charity
USE = give alms

altitude = height
USE = flying at an altitude of 10 000 meters

altruism = benevolence, generosity, unselfish concern for other's welfare
USE = an act of altruism

amid = among
USE = amid mounds of books

amphibious = able to operate in water and land
USE = frogs are amphibious

amuse = entertain
USE = Apparently these stories are meant to amuse

annex = to attach
USE = turn left to go to the annex

antagonize = harass
USE = I've no wish to antagonize him

anthrax = disease
USE = anthrax virus

apartheid = racial segregation
USE = the long-awaited dismantling of apartheid in South Africa

apt = suitable
USE = an apt comment

aristocrat = nobleman
USE = an aristocratic family

assassin = murderer
USE = She hired an assassin to kill her rival

atomize (BRITISH = atomise) = vaporize
USE = *

attire = dress
USE = appropriate attire for a wedding

audition = tryout
USE = The film director is holding auditions for a hero

aura = atmosphere, emanation
USE = an aura of mystery

authorize = grant, sanction
USE = Who authorized this expenditure?

avail = assistance
USE = Employees should avail themselves of the opportunity

avant garde = vanguard
USE = avant-garde art

barbarian = savage
USE = The walled city was attacked by barbarian hordes

battery = physical attack
USE = assault and battery

becoming = proper
USE = That's a most becoming dress

befit = to be suitable
USE = it befits for her to be the CEO

beget = produce, procreate
USE = poverty begets hunger, and hunger begets crime

bereave = rob
USE = bereaved parents

biodegradable = naturally decaying
USE = Biodegradable packaging helps reduce pollution

biopsy = removing, tissue for examination
USE = a tissue biopsy

blasphemy = insulting God
USE = to be accused of blasphemy

bliss = happiness
USE = my idea of sheer bliss

bona fide = made in good faith
USE = a bona fide resident

booty = loot
USE = to divide the booty

boycott = abstain in protest
USE = to boycott the meeting

brink = edge
USE = to the brink of failure

brook = tolerate
USE = She won't brook any criticism of her work

cabaret = night club
USE = a cabaret act.

cadet = a student of a military academy
USE = NCC cadets

calculating = scheming
USE = a very cold and calculating character

capital = most significant, pertaining to wealth
USE = capital gain tax

captivate = engross, fascinate
USE = she captivated audiences

cashmere = fine wool from Asia
USE = cashmere wool comes from Kashmir

catastrophic = disastrous
USE = catastrophic result

ceramics = pottery
USE = made of ceramics

chronicle = a history
USE = a chronicle of the Independence Movement

chronology = arrangement by time
USE = the chronology of events

circumcise = remove the foreskin
USE = he was circumcised when 6 years of age

citation = summons to appear in court
USE = The court issued a contempt citation against city council

clan = extended family
USE = the whole clan came to visit us

clone = duplicate
USE = Dolly was the first sheep clone

clout = influence
USE = the Indian maharajas have no real political clout

combine = unite, blend
USE = combined with

commodity = product
USE = commodities market

communion = fellowship
USE = a spiritual communion

compassion = kindness
USE = show a little compassion

competence = skillfulness
USE = You'll soon reach a reasonable level of competence in English

compile = collect
USE = compiling some facts and figures

comprise = To consist of
USE = an orchestra is comprised of musicians

compulsory = obligatory
USE = Wearing seat belts in cars is compulsory by law

concerted = done together
USE = take concerted action

concourse = throng
USE = There's a ticket machine in the main concourse

conducive = helping
USE = noise is not conducive to a good night's sleep

confer = To bestow
USE = An honorary doctorate was conferred on him

conference = meeting
USE = a conference on women's rights

confide = trust another (with secrets)
USE = Did you confide this to any friend

confront = challenge
USE = It's an issue we'll have to confront at some point

confuse = perplex
USE = Stop confusing the issue

consecutive = one after another
USE = the third consecutive weekend

considered = well thought out, contemplated
USE = It is my considered opinion

consortium = cartel
USE = a consortium of computer manufacturers

conspicuous = obvious
USE = He tried not to look conspicuous

conspire = plot
USE = He felt that his colleagues were conspiring together to remove him from his job.

constellation = arrangement of stars
USE = a constellation of film stars

contemplate = meditate
USE = I'm contemplating going abroad for a year

contented = satisfied
USE = a contented smile

contraction = shrinkage
USE = Cold causes contraction of the metal

contractual = related to a contract
USE = under a contractual obligation

contrast = difference, comparison
USE = a marked contrast between

controversial = subject to dispute
USE = a controversial issue

convey = communicate
USE = You don't want to convey the impression that we're not interested

convocation = gathering
USE = a university convocation

counterstrike = strike back
USE = *

court-martial = military trial
USE = he had to face a court-martial for disobeying the commanding officer

crave = desire
USE = Many young children crave attention

critique = examination, criticism
USE = a critique of the new policy

culminate = climax
USE = Their many years of research have finally culminated in a cure for the disease

curriculum = course of study
USE = the school curriculum

cyclone = storm
USE = *

czar = Russian emperor
USE = the Russian czar

de facto = actual
USE = de facto standard

deceive = trick
USE = the company deceived customers

decline = decrease in number
USE = The actor's popularity has declined

decree = official order
USE = military decree

deduce = conclude
USE = *

deduct = subtract
USE = deduct the amount and pay me the rest

deem = judge
USE = deemed university

deficit = shortage
USE = a budget deficit

deflower = despoil
USE = *

defraud = swindle
USE = The company was accused of defrauding its customers.hint

degrade = demean
USE = don't degrade woman

dehydrate = dry out
USE = feeling dehydrated

deity = a god
USE = worship deity

delinquent = negligent, culpable
USE = juvenile delinquents

demoralize = dishearten
USE = completely demoralized team

denote = signify, stand for
USE = The color red is used to denote passion or danger

depart = leave
USE = the train departs from Platform 1

deportment = behavior
USE = speech and deportment lessons

deprive = take away
USE = deprived of sleep

designate = appoint
USE = he was designated as the team captain

detain = confine
USE = A suspect was detained by the police

detract = lessen
USE = All that make-up she wears actually detracts from her beauty, I think

devastate = lay waste
USE = the city was devastated by the bombs

devise = plan
USE = devised a game plan

dictate = command
USE = the dictates of conscience

diligent = hard-working
USE = diligent about his work

discord = lack of harmony
USE = religious discord

discourse = conversation
USE = a discourse on the nature of life after death

discreet = prudent
USE = please, be discreet about it

discriminating = able to see differences
USE = discriminating shoppers

disengage = release, detach
USE = He gently disengaged his hand from hers.

disfigure = mar, ruin
USE = he was horribly disfigured by burns

dismal = gloomy
USE = a dismal performance

dismay = dread
USE = filled with dismay

dispatch = send
USE = to dispatch the letters

dispossess = take away possessions
USE = dispossessed of their homes

dissolution = disintegration
USE = the assembly was dissolved

distract = divert
USE = Don't distract her from her studies

dividend = distributed profits
USE = Dividends are sent to shareholders

dock = curtail
USE = The University has docked lecturers' pay by 20% because of their refusal to mark examination papers

don = assume, put on
USE = He donned his finest suit

double-entendre = having two meanings one of which is sexually suggestive
USE = he entertained us with double-entendre

doughty = resolute, unafraid
USE = *

draconian = harsh
USE = draconian laws

duet = twosome
USE = a duet song

ejaculate = exclaim
USE = You've got my umbrella! he ejaculated

elate = raise spirits
USE = you will feel elated on your success

electorate = voters
USE = the wishes of the electorate

elegant = refined, exquisite
USE = a very elegant suit

elite = upper-class
USE = the country's educated elite

eloquent = well-spoken
USE = an eloquent speaker

elude = evade
USE = the solution eluded them

embargo = restriction
USE = America imposed embargo on Iraq

embody = personify
USE = She embodied good sportsmanship on the playing field.

embrace = accept
USE = This was an opportunity that he would embrace

emissary = messenger
USE = the personal emissary of the Prime Minister

employ = use
USE = statistical analysis was employed to obtain these results

empower = enable, grant
USE = we empowered the employees to better help customers

enact = decree, ordain
USE = the government enacted a new law

encapsulate = condense
USE = to encapsulate the story

encyclopedia (BRITISH = encyclopaedia) = A work containing information on subjects, or exhaustive of one subject
USE = the Encyclopedia Britannica

encyclopedic (BRITISH = encyclopaedic) = comprehensive
USE = encyclopedic knowledge

endeavor (BRITISH = endeavour) = attempt, strive
USE = Engineers are endeavoring to locate the source of the problem

endocrinologist = one who studies glands of internal secretion
USE = *

endowment = property, gift
USE = The school has received an endowment of a million rupees to buy new books for the library

endure = suffer
USE = We had to endure a nine-hour delay at the airport

enfranchise = liberate
USE = *

engaging = enchanting, charming
USE = an engaging smile

engulf = overwhelm
USE = The flames rapidly engulfed the house

enlighten = inform
USE = Swami Vivekananda became enlightened

enlist = join
USE = enlist the support of local politicians

enterprise = undertaking
USE = a commercial enterprise

entourage = assemblage
USE = entourage of dancers

enviable = desirable
USE = in the enviable position

envision = imagine
USE = When do you envision finishing the project

envoy = messenger
USE = a United Nations special envoy

epic = majestic
<u>USE</u> = a talk of epic proportions

epidemic = spreading rapidly
<u>USE</u> = a flu epidemic

CD 10

episode = incident
USE = an episode of a TV serial

era = period of time
USE = the Gandhi era

err = mistake, misjudge
USE = He erred in agreeing to her appointment

erupt = burst forth
USE = the volcano erupted

eternal = endless
USE = eternal arguing

etiquette = manners
USE = social etiquette

evangelical = proselytizing
USE = the Evangelical movement

eventful = momentous
USE = an eventful journey

evolution = gradual change
USE = Darwin's theory of evolution

exact = use authority to force payment
USE = The blackmailers exacted a total of a million rupees from their victims

exacting = demanding, difficult
USE = an exacting training schedule

exclaim = shout
USE = Rubbish! he exclaimed in disgust

exclude = shut out
USE = are excluded from the club

exclusive = prohibitive
USE = an exclusive interview

exempt = excuse
USE = exempted from the tax increase

exhaustive = thorough
USE = an exhaustive study

exhibitionist = one who draws attention to himself
USE = he is an exhibitionist on the dance floor

exile = banish
USE = The king went into exile

expanse = extent of land
USE = the immense expanse of the sea

expel = drive out
USE = The new government has expelled all foreign diplomats

expose = divulge
USE = a searing exposé of police corruption

extemporize = improvise
USE = I'd lost my notes and had to extemporize

extent = scope
USE = the extent of his injuries

extract = to pull out, exact
USE = The tooth was eventually extracted

extradite = deport, deliver
USE = He will be extradited to India from Britain

fabrication = a lie
USE = The evidence he gave in court was a complete fabrication

fallacy = false belief
USE = it's a fallacy that problems disappear if you ignore them.

fatal = resulting in death
USE = the fatal shooting

feat = deed
USE = The Eiffel Tower is a remarkable feat of engineering

fertile = fruitful
USE = fertile land

font = source, fountainhead, set of type
USE = *

forthright = frank
USE = a forthright reply

fragile = Easily broken
USE = fragile crockery

fragmented = broken into fragments
USE = increasingly fragmented society

fraternity = brotherhood
USE = a means of promoting fraternity

fruitful = productive
USE = a most fruitful discussion

fuming = angry
USE = fuming at the injustice

gainful = profitable
USE = in search of gainful employment

genetics = study of heredity
USE = *

gingivitis = inflammation of the gums
USE = *

gracious = kindness
USE = a gracious smile

gradient = incline, rising by degrees
USE = a steep gradient

gradual = by degrees
USE = a gradual improvement

gratitude = thankfulness
USE = to show her gratitude

habituate = accustom
USE = *

havoc = destruction
USE = The storm wreaked havoc in the garden

heed = follow advice
USE = failing to heed warnings

herald = harbinger
USE = The president's speech heralds a new era in foreign policy

hermit = one who lives in solitude
USE = *

heuristic = teaching device or method
USE = *

heyday = glory days
USE = In their heyday

holograph = written entirely by hand
USE = *

homely = plain
USE = The hotel was homely and comfortable

humanities = languages and literature
USE = more interested in the humanities than the sciences

hyperactive = overactive
USE = Hyperactive children

hypertension = elevated blood pressure
USE = a new drug for hypertension

hypocritical = deceiving , two-faced
USE = Their accusations of corruption are hypocritical - they have been just as corrupt themselves

hypoglycemic (BRITISH = hypoglycaemic) = low blood sugar
USE = As a diabetic she was accustomed to the occasional hypoglycemic attack

immunity = exemption from prosecution
USE = He was granted immunity from prosecution

impartial = not biased
USE = an impartial judgment

impede = hinder
USE = a broken-down car is impeding the flow of traffic

imperceptible = slight, intangible
USE = imperceptible changes

imposition = intrusion
USE = the imposition of the death penalty

in toto = in full, entirely
USE = The available information amounts to very little in toto

inadvisable = not recommended
USE = Weight-lifting is inadvisable if you have a weak heart

inaudible = cannot be heard
USE = The traffic noise made her voice inaudible

inborn = innate
USE = an inborn tendency

incest = sexual activity between family members
USE = a victim of incest

incidental = insignificant, minor
USE = incidental details

incinerate = burn
USE = to incinerate waste

incision = cut
USE = The surgeon made a small incision

incomparable = peerless
USE = incomparable beauty

incompatibility = inability to live in harmony
USE = An incompatibility problem prevents the two pieces of software from being used together

inconsiderate = thoughtless
USE = Our neighbors are very inconsiderate

inconspicuous = not noticeable
USE = At parties, he always stands in a corner and tries to look inconspicuous

incorporate = combine
USE = This aircraft incorporates several new safety features

indecent = offensive
USE = an indecent act

indiscreet = Lacking wise judgment
USE = In an indiscreet moment

industrious = hard-working
USE = an industrious worker

infantry = foot soldiers
USE = heavy infantry unit

inflammatory = incendiary
USE = inflammatory speech

infuse = inspire, instill
USE = Her arrival infused the children with enthusiasm

initiation = induction ceremony
USE = the initiation of divorce proceedings

innovative = new, useful idea
USE = innovative ideas

installment (BRITISH = instalment) = portion
USE = pay each installment on time

instant = at once
USE = instant tea, instant coffee

intangible = Not perceptible to the touch
USE = charisma is an intangible quality

integration = unification
USE = cultural integration

intensive = extreme
USE = an intensive course in English

intercept = prevent
USE = The police intercepted a shipment of fake drugs

interstate = between states
USE = the interstate highway system

intricate = complex
USE = an intricate design

intrigue = plot, mystery
USE = people have been intrigued by

inventive = cleaver, resourceful
USE = He is very inventive

inviolate = sacred
USE = For centuries the tomb lay inviolate

invocation = calling on God
USE = *

irate = angry
USE = irate phone calls

irrational = illogical
USE = It's totally irrational

jest = joke
USE = Would I jest about something so important

jubilant = in high spirits
USE = The fans were jubilant about India's victory

jurisdiction = domain
USE = sales are subject to Mumbai jurisdiction only

justify = excuse, mitigate
USE = I can't really justify taking another day off work

Koran = holy book of Islam
USE = *

lactic = derived from milk
USE = lactic acid

laurels = fame
USE = the laurels must surely go to the director of the play

layman = nonprofessional
USE = in layman's terms

liable = responsible
USE = you will be liable for the loss

lieutenant = one acts in place of another
USE = second lieutenant

litigate = contest
USE = you'll have to litigate to get your rights

logistics = means of supplying troops
USE = the logistics of the whole aid operation

lure = entice
USE = the lure of fame

magisterial = arbitrary, dictatorial
USE = *

magnum opus = masterpiece
USE = the painting is considered to be his magnum opus

maladjusted = disturbed
USE = maladjusted children

malevolence = bad intent, malice
USE = an act of great malevolence

mania = madness
USE = a sudden mania for exercise

manslaughter = killing someone without malice
USE = She was sentenced to five years imprisonment for manslaughter

manuscript = unpublished book
<u>USE</u> = the 400-page manuscript

maternity = motherhood
<u>USE</u> = maternity leave

memoir = autobiography
<u>USE</u> = She has written a memoir

memorabilia = things worth remembering
<u>USE</u> = Cricket memorabilia

memorandum = note
<u>USE</u> = memorandum of understanding

migrate = travel
<u>USE</u> = Many Indians migrate to America

milk = extract
<u>USE</u> = The directors milked the company of several million dollars

mince = chop, moderate
<u>USE</u> = not mince your words

minute = very small
<u>USE</u> = a minute quantity

misappropriation = use dishonestly
<u>USE</u> = He was charged with forgery, embezzlement and misappropriation of union funds

miscarry = abort
<u>USE</u> = Sadly, she miscarried eight weeks into the pregnancy

mnemonics = that which aids the memory
<u>USE</u> = mnemonics help you remember better

mobilize = assemble for action
<u>USE</u> = to mobilize voter support

mobocracy = rule by mob
<u>USE</u> = *

module = unit
<u>USE</u> = The full computer program is made up of several modules

molest = bother
<u>USE</u> = The girl had been molested

morale = spirit, confidence
<u>USE</u> = the team's high morale

morphine = painkilling drug
USE = he took morphine for pain

mosque = a place of worship
USE = he prayed in the mosque

motive = reason
USE = a motive for lying

motto = slogan, saying
USE = Our motto is your service

multitude = throng
USE = a multitude of problems

murmur = mutter, mumble
USE = "I love you", she murmured

mutiny = rebellion
USE = rumors of mutiny among the troops

mythical = fictitious
USE = a mythical hero

narrate = tell, recount
USE = can you narrate the event for us

naturalize = grant citizenship
USE = a naturalized US citizen

negate = cancel
USE = increase in our profits has been negated by

neurotic = disturbed
USE = She's neurotic about her weight

nimble = spry, quick
USE = nimble fingers

nominate = propose
USE = He was nominated for the post of chairman

nominee = candidate
USE = All nominees for Treasurer will be considered

notable = remarkable, noteworthy
USE = a notable achievement

noted = famous
USE = a noted writer

nouveau riche = newly rich
USE = *

nuisance = annoyance
USE = power failure was a real nuisance

nymph = goddess
USE = *

objectivity = impartiality
USE = true objectivity in a critic is impossible

oblige = compel
USE = The law obliges companies to pay decent wages to their employees

observant = watchful
USE = he was very observant

obtain = gain possession
USE = to obtain permission

octogenarian = person in eighties
USE = his grandfather is an octogenarian

ocular = related to the eye, optic, visual
USE = *

officiate = supervise
USE = A priest officiated at the wedding

offset = counterbalance
USE = The extra cost of traveling to work is offset by the lower price of houses here

omnibus = collection, compilation
USE = the omnibus edition

operative = working
USE = The agreement will not become operative until all members have signed

oppress = persecute
USE = oppressed by a ruthless dictator

oppressive = burdensome
USE = an oppressive government

opt = decide, choose
USE = he opted for early retirement

orderly = neat
USE = She put the letters in three orderly piles

otherworldly = spiritual
USE = The children in the picture look delicate and otherworldly

ovation = applause
USE = standing ovation

overrule = disallow
USE = In tennis, the umpire can overrule the line judge

overwhelm = overpower
USE = overwhelmed by grief

pact = agreement
USE = a free-trade pact

pagan = heathen, ungodly
USE = a pagan festival

page = attendant
USE = *

pageant = exhibition, show
USE = a beauty pageant

pains = labor
USE = she was in labor pains

pantry = storeroom
USE = get tea from the office pantry

paranoid = obsessively suspicious, demented
USE = He started feeling paranoid and was convinced his boss was going to fire him

paranormal = supernatural
USE = paranormal powers

parcel = package
USE = a food parcel

parrot = mimic
USE = she just parrots anything that her mom says

partition = division
USE = partition of India in 1947

paternal = Fatherly
USE = paternal grandfather

pathogen = agent causing disease
USE = a dangerous pathogen

pawn = pledge
USE = Of all items pawned, jewelry is the most common

peaked = wan, pale, haggard
USE = looked a bit peaked

peculiar = unusual
USE = a peculiar smell

peculiarity = characteristic
USE = we all have our little peculiarities

peddle = sell
USE = peddle drugs

CD 11

pen = write
USE = he penned the story

per se = in itself
USE = Research shows that it is not divorce per se that harms children, but the continuing conflict between parents.

perceptive = discerning
USE = perceptive insights

perfectionist = purist, precisionist
USE = don't be a perfectionist

perforate = puncture
USE = a perforated eardrum

perish = die
USE = Three hundred people perished in the earthquake

perishable = decomposable
USE = perishable food

permutation = reordering
USE = permutations of the numbers

perpendicular = at right angles
USE = the nearly perpendicular side of the mountain

perpetuate = cause to continue
USE = perpetuate the violence

persecute = harass
USE = Religious minorities were persecuted

persevere = persist, endure
USE = persevere in your efforts for great success

persona = social façade
USE = his public persona

personify = embody, exemplify
USE = In Greek myth, love is personified by the goddess Aphrodite

personnel = employees
USE = military personnel

persuasive = convincing
USE = a persuasive speaker

pertain = to relate
USE = the parts of the proposals that pertain to local issue

peruse = read carefully
USE = He opened a newspaper and began to peruse

pessimist = cynic
USE = Don't be such a pessimist

petite = small
USE = She was dark and petite

petition = request
USE = I signed a petition against

phenomenal = unusual natural events, or extraordinary
USE = a phenomenal success

philanthropic = charitable
USE = a philanthropic society

philatelist = stamp collector
USE = *

philosophical = contemplative
USE = philosophical writings

physique = frame, musculature
USE = a very powerful, muscular physique

piecemeal = one at a time
USE = everything is being done piecemeal

pine = languish
USE = pined away and died

pitiable = miserable, wretched
USE = a pitiable state of affairs

pivotal = crucial
USE = a pivotal role

pleasantry = banter, persiflage
USE = After exchanging pleasantries

plentiful = Abundant
USE = a plentiful supply of

plight = sad situation
USE = the plight of the poor

plutonium = radioactive material
USE = a bomb made of plutonium

polychromatic = many-colored
USE = *

ponder = muse, reflect
USE = to ponder her next move

posthaste (BRITISH = post-haste) = hastily
USE = They traveled posthaste to Rome to collect the award

potent = powerful
USE = a potent drug

preconception = prejudgment, prejudice
USE = without too many preconceptions

predisposed = inclined
USE = genetically predisposed to cancer

prefabricated = ready-built
USE = a prefabricated house

prefect = magistrate
USE = appointed as Prefect

preference = choice
USE = preference is for tea

preferment = promotion
USE = *

preliminary = introductory
USE = Preliminary results

prenatal = before birth
USE = the prenatal clinic

prerequisite = requirement
USE = a prerequisite for success

presentable = acceptable, well-mannered
USE = was looking quite presentable

preside = direct, chair
USE = to preside over the public enquiry

pressing = urgent
USE = a pressing issue

presume = deduce
USE = I presume that they're not coming

presuppose = assume
USE = All this presupposes that he'll get the job he wants

pretense (BRITISH = pretence) = affection, excuse
USE = She made absolutely no pretence of being interested.

prevailing = common, current
USE = the prevailing attitude

prick = puncture
USE = She pricked the balloon with a pin

primal = first, beginning
USE = primal fears

primate = head, master
USE = He was made the Roman Catholic Primate of All Ireland

princely = regal, generous
USE = a princely childhood

problematic = uncertain
USE = problematic situation

procedure = method
USE = correct procedure

proceeds = profit
USE = The proceeds of today's festival will go to local charities

proclaim = announce
USE = All the countries have proclaimed their loyalty to the alliance

procreate = beget
USE = the right to marry and procreate

prodigy = a person with extraordinary ability or talent
USE = a child prodigy

profess = affirm
USE = She professes not to be interested in money

profiteer = extortionist
USE = a war profiteer

profound = deep, knowledgeable
USE = profound wisdom

proliferate = increase rapidly
USE = Coaching institutes have proliferated in the last ten years

prolong = lengthen in time
USE = decided to prolong our stay

prompt = induce
USE = The speech has prompted an angry response

propaganda = publicity
USE = political propaganda

prophet = prognosticator
USE = the words of the prophet

proportionate = commensurate
USE = Weight is proportional to size

proposition = offer, proposal
USE = a business proposition

proprietor = manager, owner
USE = a newspaper proprietor

prospective = expected, imminent
USE = prospective employers

prospectus = brochure
USE = impressive prospectus

proverb = maxim
USE = an old proverb

proverbial = well-known
USE = his proverbial good humor

providence = foresight, divine protection
USE = divine providence

province = bailiwick, district
USE = the province of Rajasthan

provisional = temporary
USE = a provisional certificate

provisory = conditional
USE = *hint

provocative = titillating
USE = a provocative question

psychopath = madman
USE = *

psychotic = demented
USE = a psychotic disorder

puberty = adolescence
USE = At puberty, girls begin to menstruate

pulp = paste, mush
USE = Mash the bananas to a pulp

pulpit = platform, priesthood
USE = the priest spoke from the pulpit

pun = wordplay
USE = a well-known joke based on a pun

purposeful = determined
USE = He has a quiet, purposeful air

pursuant = following, according
USE = pursuant to an order

pygmy = dwarf
USE = a political pygmy

pyrotechnics = fireworks
USE = pyrotechnics show on the Independence Day

quantum = quantity, particle
USE = a quantum leap

quarter = residence
USE = government quarters

questionnaire = interrogation
USE = fill in a questionnaire

quota = a share or proportion
USE = the usual quota

rapidity = speed
USE = *

reap = harvest
USE = reap the benefit

recede = move back
USE = The painful memories gradually receded in her mind

recital = performance
USE = a piano recital

recitation = recital, lesson
USE = recitation of some poem

recoil = flinch, retreat
USE = I recoiled from the smell

recollect = remember
USE = As far as I can recollect

recoup = recover
USE = recouped his losses

recuperation = recovery
USE = he fell from the horse and the recuperation took three months

redoubt = fort
USE = the last redoubt of upper-class privilege

reel = stagger
USE = She hit him so hard that he reeled backwards

refined = purified, cultured
USE = refined oil

refrain = abstain
USE = Please refrain from smoking

regrettable = lamentable
USE = a deeply regrettable mistake

rehash = repeat
USE = His new book is just a rehash

reincarnation = rebirth
USE = Hindus and Buddhists believe in reincarnation

rejoice = celebrate
USE = She rejoiced in her good fortune

relapse = recurrence of illness
USE = relapse of malaria

relentless = unstoppable
USE = relentless criticism

relic = antique
USE = During the dig, the archeological team found some relics from the Stone Age

repatriate = to send back to the native land
USE = The government repatriated him because he had no visa

repulsive = repugnant
USE = I think rats are repulsive

repute = esteem
USE = a place of ill repute

requisition = order
USE = The staff made a requisition for

reside = dwell
USE = My family now resides in India

resigned = accepting of a situation
USE = a resigned look

resilience = ability to recover from an illness
USE = *

resort = recourse
USE = He got back the money legally, without resort to violence

resourceful = inventive, skillful
USE = a resourceful manager

respectively = in order
USE = first and third position respectively

resurgence = revival
USE = resurgence in demand

retainer = advance fee
USE = he paid the lawyer Rs 1,000 as retainer

revamp = recast
USE = We revamped all the management system

revenue = income
USE = revenues fell dramatically

revision = new version
USE = These proposals will need a lot of revision

revive = renew
USE = to revive someone's hopes

rheumatism = inflammation
USE = suffer from rheumatism

rogue = scoundrel
USE = a rogue state

rouse = awaken
USE = He roused himself and got back to work

rudiment = beginning
USE = rudiments of an experiment

sabbatical = vacation
USE = sabbatical leave

sabotage = treason, destruction
USE = attempt to sabotage the ceasefire

sacred cow = idol, taboo
USE = the sacred cow of parliamentary democracy

saddle = encumber, burden, strain
USE = put a saddle on the horse

safari = expedition
USE = to go on safari

sage = wise person
USE = sage advice

salvation = redemption
USE = a marriage beyond salvation

sans = without
USE = *

satanic = pertaining to the Devil
USE = a satanic cult

savvy = perceptive
USE = business savvy

scant = inadequate, meager
USE = scant regard for the truth

scheme = plot
USE = All her ministers were scheming against her

scorn = disdain, reject
USE = She has nothing but scorn for him

scoundrel = unprincipled person
USE = a heartless scoundrel

scruples = misgivings
USE = Robin Hood had no scruples about robbing the rich to give to the poor

scrutinize = examine closely
USE = He scrutinized the men's faces carefully

secure = make safe
USE = Endangered species need to be kept secure from poachers

sedation = state of calm
USE = She's under strong sedation

seduce = lure
USE = I was seduced by the low price

seismic = pertaining to earthquakes
USE = seismic activity

self-effacing = modest
USE = The captain was typically self-effacing, giving credit to the other players

semantics = study of word meanings
USE = semantics describes what words mean

seniority = privilege due to length of service
USE = promotion will be based on seniority

sensational = outstanding
USE = a sensational sports car

sensible = wise
USE = a sensible answer

sensory = relating to senses
USE = sensory appeal

sensualist = epicure
USE = *

serene = peaceful
USE = She has a lovely serene face

session = meeting
USE = The parliamentary session

sever = cut in two
USE = Her foot was severed from her leg in a car accident

shortcomings = deficiencies
USE = Like any political system, it has its shortcomings

signatory = signer
USE = are signatories to

singular = unique
USE = singular grace and beauty

site = location
USE = the site for the new hospital

slate = list of candidates
USE = he is slated to be the next captain of the cricket team

snub = ignore
USE = she felt snubbed

socialite = one who is prominent in society
USE = a wealthy socialite

sociology = study of society
USE = a degree in sociology

solemn = serious, somber
USE = a solemn face

solemnity = seriousness
USE = the solemnity of a funeral service

specimen = sample
USE = a collection of rare insect specimens

speculate = conjecture
USE = to speculate on the cause of train crash

spindle = shaft
USE = *

spirited = lively
USE = high-spirited

spite = malice, grudge
USE = just out of spite

splurge = indulge
USE = I feel like splurging on a new dress

statute = regulation
USE = a new statute on taxes

staunch = loyal
USE = staunch supporter

stealth = secrecy, covertness
USE = These thieves operate with stealth

stenography = shorthand
USE = *

stimulate = excite
USE = stimulate students to think

stipulate = specify, arrange
USE = The law stipulates that

stole = long scarf
USE = a mink stole

striking = impressive, attractive
USE = her striking looks

strive = endeavor
USE = strive to live up to the expectations

submit = yield
USE = We protested about the changes, but in the end we had to submit

subordinate = lower in rank
USE = a subordinate role

subside = diminish
USE = the violence will soon subside

subsidize = financial assistance
USE = to subsidize the training

suffice = adequate
USE = I think that should suffice

suggestive = thought-provoking, risque
USE = The amplified sounds are suggestive of dolphins chatting to each other under the sea

summon = call for, arraign
USE = to summon reinforcements

superb = excellent
USE = a superb performance

superintend = supervise
USE = Her job is to superintend the production process

superlative = superior
<u>USE</u> = a superlative restaurant

Free Download
MP3 File of CD #1:

www.FranklinVocab.com/exec/free.php

Available MP3 Download of
Words from All 11 CDs

www.FranklinVocab.com/exec

Support Email:
FranklinVocab@gmail.com

Printed in Great Britain
by Amazon.co.uk, Ltd.,
Marston Gate.